G000291626

'*Wrestling with My Thoughts* is an extra
sion to eating disorders to mania to ps
experienced a vast amount of mental i
story with almost excruciating honesty.

'*Wrestling with My Thoughts* is a painful read. I had to stop several
times to process the things I had read. But it is also a deeply needed
book. Sharon writes from a unique perspective not only as someone
with mental illness, but also as a medical professional. It is a perspective that is incredibly helpful, meaning that we are brought into
the story on a personal level with Sharon, but are also educated
about the illnesses themselves. Sharon is very honest about the
treatments she received, and highlights the importance of help
while also admitting its shortcomings.

'One of the difficult but wonderful things about this book is the
fact that it doesn't have an easy or a happy ending. Sharon has con-
tinuing struggles, as we all do. However, it is a glorious picture of
God holding on to a dearly beloved child, even as he allows incredibly
hard things to happen to her. He remains faithful, forgiving and
good throughout it all, and it is a beautiful thing to read about
Sharon's return to him. It is a story of incredible humbling, and one
about accepting the life that God has for each of us, no matter if it's
the one we expected or not.'
Ruth van den Broek, blogger and sufferer

'With courageous humility, Sharon Hastings has given us a rare
privilege: sharing her experience as a Christian with mental illness.
Her story is honest, at times heart-rending, but eventually hopeful.
This book will pass on that hope to many struggling Christians who
can easily feel excluded and forgotten. It will also equip the church
better to understand and care for those who appear to be the weaker
members of the body – but upon whom God has bestowed greater
honour. Read this book, witness living faith, and see why God
esteems those weakened through mental ill-health.'
Dr Andrew Collins, consultant psychiatrist and biblical
counsellor

'In this remarkable book, Sharon Hastings unfolds with unflinching honesty the devastating effects of severe mental illness on her life and hopes. A qualified doctor, she tells of the heartbreaking loss of being unable to practise her profession. Her medical knowledge adds an extra layer of poignancy to the narrative. And, as a Christian, she testifies to the particular spiritual challenges presented by the relentless attacks on her mind. To a reader who has not suffered mental illness, the book is revelatory, and even shocking. Fed by Scripture, enormous courage and, above all, the love of Christ, it is a victory for hope in the midst of darkness, a unique and profound work of spirituality, and, in the end, a deeply moving love story.'
Gordon McConville, Professor of Old Testament Theology, University of Gloucestershire

'It is a strange truth that when people generalize how to handle suffering, they often compound it, but when people relate the specifics of their own suffering, they give untold confidence and inspiration to others, even when in very different circumstances. Sharon Hastings' story is heartbreaking but very powerful. It is a bravely honest testimony to the goodness of God, the vital support of loving friends and the resilience and perseverance of a remarkable person. To be invited to walk alongside her during some of the darkest periods of her life is a rare privilege indeed.'
Mark Meynell, author, trainer, blogger, and Director for Langham Preaching

'What an incredible story and what an incredible woman . . . Severe mental illness is a difficult and painful topic, but Sharon writes with immense courage and clarity about her experiences. Writing from both a personal and a clinical perspective, she offers a unique insight into depression, bipolar, EDNOS and schizoaffective disorder. I was inspired, challenged and profoundly moved by her story – and you will be too. Raw and powerful, this is a book that demands to be read.'
Emma Scrivener, author, blogger and speaker

'Sharon's story is raw and compelling. It engenders hope that true grace can be found in the midst of deep suffering. Her battle with mental illness has been characterized by a gritty perseverance which forms real character. As she testifies herself, this is made possible by the fact that she is being held by God even when all seems lost. This book can be of much help to believers who struggle with the shame and stigma of profound mental disorder. It provides wise advice for churches seeking to respond well to those who are afflicted with severe psychological conditions. It is to the immense benefit of others that Sharon has been able bravely to recount her journey, and that her intense internal wrestling has not been in vain.'
Dr Ken Yeow, consultant psychiatrist

WRESTLING WITH MY THOUGHTS

Sharon Hastings

WRESTLING WITH MY THOUGHTS

A doctor with severe mental illness discovers strength

Sharon Hastings

INTER-VARSITY PRESS
36 Causton Street, London SW1P 4ST, England
Email: ivp@ivpbooks.com
Website: www.ivpbooks.com

Unless otherwise noted, Scripture quotations are taken from The Holy Bible, New
International Version (Anglicized edition). Copyright © 1979, 1984, 2011 by Biblica.
Used by permission of Hodder & Stoughton Ltd, an Hachette UK company. All rights
reserved.'NIV' is a registered trademark of Biblica. UK trademark number 1448790.

Some Scripture quotations are from *THE MESSAGE*. Copyright © by Eugene
H. Peterson 1993, 1994, 1995, 1996, 2000, 2001, 2002. Used by permission of
NavPress Publishing Group.

The publisher and author acknowledge with thanks permission to reproduce
extracts from the following:
Lyrics from 'All for Jesus' by Robin Mark used by kind permission.
Extracts from 'Let You Go' by Ruth Trimble used by kind permission.
The Problem of Pain by C. S. Lewis © copyright C. S. Lewis Pte Ltd 1940.
The Collected Letters of C. S. Lewis Volume II by C. S. Lewis
© copyright C. S. Lewis Pte Ltd 2004.
Every effort has been made to seek permission to use copyright material reproduced
in this book. The publisher apologizes for those cases where permission might not have
been sought and, if notified, will formally seek permission at the earliest opportunity.

First published 2020

British Library Cataloguing-in-Publication Data
A catalogue record for this book is available from the British Library.

ISBN: 978–1–78974–088–2
eBook ISBN: 978–1–78974–089–9

Set in 11/14pt Minion Pro

Typeset in Great Britain by CRB Associates, Potterhanworth, Lincolnshire
Printed in Great Britain by Ashford Colour Press Ltd, Gosport, Hampshire

*Inter-Varsity Press publishes Christian books that are true to the Bible and that
communicate the gospel, develop discipleship and strengthen the church for its mission
in the world.*

*IVP originated within the Inter-Varsity Fellowship, now the Universities and Colleges
Christian Fellowship, a student movement connecting Christian Unions in universities
and colleges throughout Great Britain, and a member movement of the International
Fellowship of Evangelical Students. Website: www.uccf.org.uk. That historic association
is maintained, and all senior IVP staff and committee members subscribe to the
UCCF Basis of Faith.*

For Olivia

How long, LORD? Will you forget me for ever?
How long will you hide your face from me?
How long must I wrestle with my thoughts
and day after day have sorrow in my heart?
(Psalm 13:1–2)

Mental pain is less dramatic than physical pain, but it is more
common and also more hard to bear. The frequent attempt
to conceal mental pain increases the burden: it is easier to say
'My tooth is aching' than to say 'My heart is broken.'
(C. S. Lewis, *The Problem of Pain*)[1]

Contents

Contents

Preface and acknowledgments

This is the story of my personal journey through severe mental illness. I have been careful to ensure that I do not tell anyone else's story. The people you will meet as my fellow patients, and even some of my friends, are composite characters, so if you recognize anyone, it is by coincidence. Names and identifying characteristics of medical staff and institutions have also been changed.

Everything I have recorded actually happened, but in some places I have simplified the sequence of events, as to recount every episode as it occurred would take many more pages than this book will allow. The medical details included are correct at the time of writing.

Similarly, while I can recall much of the dialogue, please remember that some of these events took place more than ten years ago, so I have needed to use an author's creative licence where the memories are a little vaguer, while remaining as true to the story as possible.

The ultimate goal of this book is to bring understanding of severe mental illness to the church today, and to reduce some of the stigma that sufferers face. With each page, I have prayed for inspiration, and I trust that what I have written illuminates something new and helpful.

Many people have helped me along my writing journey. I would particularly like to acknowledge:

Rob, my fellow writer, for understanding what it takes to complete a manuscript, and for never giving up on me.

Olivia, for thirteen years of daily phone calls from California, for praying, for always knowing what is needed to sustain me, and for her unfailing love. Peter, her husband, for educating me, fostering my gifts, and never giving up on me.

My parents, for their love and for exposing me to the truths of Scripture from early childhood.

'Dr Oates', without whose advocacy and support I would not be here to write this book.

Anna, for conceiving the idea for a book and encouraging me throughout the writing process.

Emma, Gordon, Helen, Andrew, Claire, Olivia, Anna, Avril and Uel, for reading my chapters as they came together, and for the feedback which helped shape my book.

Eleanor, my wonderful editor at IVP, whose insights and expertise have been invaluable, and who visited me in hospital to keep the dream alive even when I was not well enough to write.

Jen and Heather, for their practical support – transport, meals for Rob – so helpful when I was in hospital, and Mum for doing all the ironing.

My GPs, the Community Mental Health Team, the Home Treatment Team and all the staff of the Downe Mental Health Inpatient Unit, for keeping me as well as possible, and for encouraging me to write as therapy.

The staff of Caffè Nero, who had my soya lattes ready before I could set up my laptop (and a few people who gave me Nero vouchers to fuel my writing – you know who you are).

Pastors and ministers, Baptist and Presbyterian, whose visits and teaching encouraged me through the dark times and kept me focused on the Lord.

Soli Deo Gloria.

Introduction
Deep joy

Droplets of water glistened in the early evening sunlight, spraying the stage as the two Jonathans – Jonathan my pastor and Jonathan my friend – plunged me into the baptismal tank and pulled me up again. It was a symbol – the pinnacle of my Christian life to date. I had 'died in Christ and risen with him', I was cleansed, my sins were forgiven . . . and now this church congregation, brimming with friends and family, knew all about it. I dripped water. I dripped hope. I dripped freedom. I could feel my face beaming with joy as my composure gave way to spontaneous bubbles of laughter.

I took the towel from my best friend (whose radiant smile now mirrored mine), wrapped myself in it and nearly fell off the stage in my rush to get into the side room to change and come back again. Now in dry clothes, I returned to the stage, where one of the Jonathans welcomed me and read a verse – my baptismal verse, Romans 15:13: 'May the God of hope fill you with all joy and peace as you trust in him, so that you may overflow with hope by the power of the Holy Spirit.' Hope. Joy. Peace. Yes, yes, yes. The Holy Spirit was at work and I was overflowing indeed.

The pianist struck up a few chords, and I quickly took my place in the Praise Group. I had chosen all the hymns for the evening, but this was the most important one of all. If I had shared my story in words before my baptism, now I would share it in song. 'Jesus, all for Jesus', Robin Mark's simple melody, had become so precious, so dear to my heart in recent months, reflecting everything that had been motivating me as I prepared for baptism. From now on I was risen with Christ and I would give my everything for him: 'Jesus, all for Jesus, all I am and have and ever hope to be.'[1] This was what I wanted people to understand by the symbol enacted.

I sang my heart out. No false earnestness here; I was taken up by the moment, transported to a new place in my Christian experience, wanting to express my joy in all its fullness and state my intentions with Robin's easy clarity. Especially when we came to the second verse: 'All of my ambitions, hopes and plans, I surrender these into your hands.'

Here I was, a third-year medical student, well on the way to becoming a doctor, wanting to hand that ambition completely over to the God I loved. I had chosen a caring vocation, driven by a desire to 'do something for him'. I was in good company: there were literally a couple of dozen doctors in (what was then) a smallish university-area church. I had plenty of excellent examples to follow. Now I wanted them – and everyone else there – to know that I was open to whatever God would have me do for him.

Now, at that stage I didn't really know for sure what speciality I would choose. General practice, perhaps? But right then I was open to obstetrics, to orthopaedics, to psychiatry even, if that was what God desired. I had always had thoughts about mission abroad; I was willing to go to Entebbe, to Caracas, to Azerbaijan – literally anywhere – or to stay at home if that was what would further God's Kingdom. I felt excited . . . driven . . . passionate about surrendering to God's plan.

'For it's only in your will that I am free,' we sang on. I had never been so sure that I was in God's will. How could I not be? Here I was, proclaiming my faith and commitment to him in a public arena, believing in my head that I had risen with Christ at the point of giving my life to him. I knew deep in my heart that demonstrating this symbolically had changed me too. My spirit soared, my soul yearned for more of God. I was free, and the Holy Spirit was resting on me.

'All of my ambitions, hopes and plans, I surrender these into your hands.'

But within three years, I would be a detained patient in a psychiatric hospital and denied a licence to practise as a doctor by the General Medical Council because I was 'floridly psychotic'.

Would I have sung my heart out if I'd known *that*?

1

Too numb to pray
Wrestling with thoughts of darkness

The sprawl of Los Angeles stretches out below the poolside veranda, hazy in the evening August sun. We're sitting on a swing seat, sipping tea while dinner cooks and rocking gently backwards and forwards.

The silence between us weighs heavily for a while.

Olivia's brow crinkles. 'There's something really wrong, isn't there?'

I examine my newly painted toenails.

'I've wondered for a while. I mean, you weren't going to class, and there was all this back pain, and the not sleeping . . . and then how you behaved when Janie was here . . . I was mad at first, but then . . .'

I look out towards the downtown skyscrapers in the distance and slowly shake my head.

'Sharon, do you think you're depressed?'

The 'D' word. I've pondered it for a while, but I've never been able to say it out loud.

I pause, then nod. I feel like I should maybe cry, but I'm numb.

'I think you are.'

My aunt sets her tea to one side and clasps her hands tightly.

'Sharon, I need to know because I've been leaving you alone: are you having any dark thoughts?'

I knew that was coming. Yes, all the time. I'm consumed by darkness. It swirls about me and rounds my shoulders. It steals my thoughts and hurts my neck.

'Sometimes.'

'Do you ever think about ending it all?'

What do I say?

'You can tell me. It's okay.'

I speak away from her to my left.

'Yes.'

She says nothing, but takes my hand.

'You're going to come to work with me tomorrow. I can't let you stay here . . . The pool . . .'

I know. The pool.

'Sharon, would you talk to my friend Julia? She's a therapist and I'd like to know what she thinks about how you're feeling. I value her opinion. She's wise.'

'When?'

'I don't know. I'll call her in the morning, see when she has a slot.'

'Okay.'

I sigh. I do want to talk to someone – someone I don't know, someone who can help me understand this – this dark presence with me.

Olivia looks at me and purses her lips, then relaxes them.

'You're gonna be okay, kiddo. I'm with you. And I think Julia will be a help to you.'

I nod.

'You hungry?'

I'm not. I don't feel like I could even swallow soup.

'. . . cos I think dinner's ready. If you don't feel like it, I'll just dish up a little for you.'

I get up from the seat in assent.

* * *

The next day, I go to work with Olivia.

She has to see her patients, of course, but her nurses are really kind to me. They give me some filing to do, which saves me making conversation, and there's zucchini (courgette) cake at tea break. No one asks any questions and I suspect that Olivia has told them something about why I'm here – she has to have done – but I don't care. I'm just glad that someone has taken charge of things. Of me.

At lunch, Olivia takes me to the canteen in the hospital across the way. She walks quickly, as all the doctors seem to do. We share one of those huge deli sandwiches with ham and pickle, one wedge each. I try to eat mine even though it keeps sticking in my throat.

'I've spoken to Julia.'

My heart skips a beat.

'She's going to fit you in at 10.30 tomorrow. I have the morning off, remember, so I can drive you over. Is that okay?'

'Mm-hmm.'

'She's really good, Sharon. I wouldn't take you otherwise. I trust her.'

I nod. I trust Olivia. She trusts Julia. I guess I trust Julia too. I have to.

'Thanks for sorting it.'

'Of course.'

Her bleeper goes off. We have to run, she to the labour and delivery suite, I to my filing, under several pairs of gentle, watchful eyes.

* * *

At 8 am, we take the dogs for a walk in the canyon. It's beautiful – dappled light on the winding path, ancient trees to either side – but I don't really register it.

Olivia exchanges pleasantries with other dog owners, and I try to force a smile, but aside from that we are both quiet. When it's time to turn, Olivia pours some water into a collapsible dish for the dogs and hands me a bottle too. It's hot and we sit down on a log for a second.

'You need to be honest with her – with Julia.'

'I know.'

'We need to know how to help you.'

I nod.

Olivia pulls me towards her and envelops me in a hug. I feel safe for a second, but the darkness is still there.

'Thanks.'

'It's okay.'

* * *

Julia's office is about half an hour's drive away and I mostly look out of the window. My stomach is churning.

'This is it.'

We cross a courtyard with leafy trellises surrounding it and climb an outdoor stairway to the second level, where we see Julia's name and credentials on a plaque by a door. Olivia knocks and an attractive, middle-aged lady with dark hair – not unlike Olivia – opens it.

'Good morning, Olivia. And you must be Sharon. Nice to meet you.'

'Hi, Julia. How are you? Sharon, I'm going to leave you here, okay?'

Julia fixes my gaze for a second, then turns back to my aunt.

'Okay, goodbye, Olivia. See you at 11.30?'

'I'll be here.'

Julia ushers me in and shows me a comfortable seat. There's a Star of David above her desk and a picture of the Santa Monica mountains on the wall by the door.

I twiddle my thumbs for a second and screw up my nose, then look at the floor.

Julia is kind, like Olivia said. Her voice runs like honey and her expression is open and warm.

She asks me a lot of questions – familiar questions, the questions I learnt to ask in my psychiatry placement when someone presented with low mood. Not questions I ever expected to be asked of me.

How are you feeling in your spirits? Are you finding enjoyment in anything? How is your concentration . . . your motivation? How are your relationships going? Have you been more tearful than usual? How is your appetite . . . your sleep . . . your libido? What sort of things are filling your thoughts? What are your energy levels like? Have you felt like withdrawing from your friends?

And then the big ones.

How do you feel about going back to medical school? Do you have hope for the future? Would you say that you ever think life isn't worth living?

I answer as best I can. Everything is a blur. I can't think. The words I want are just beyond my grasp.

But she nods a lot and sits forward, leaning her ear towards me. I feel as though she really cares, and it makes me want to cry, but I can't.

She takes a quick glance at the clock and I know that our time must be nearly up.

'Sharon, your aunt thinks you are depressed. Would you agree?'

'Mm-hmm. I guess.'

'Well, I do too. And I don't think this is mild depression; I think you're quite severely unwell. You're going to need some professional help, and I think we should make sure it's in place before you go home . . .'

I don't hear any more. When I go home? But I can't go home. It's okay to be depressed in America where everyone talks about their feelings and every second person has a therapist. But in Belfast? And as a medical student?

I gather myself.

'I know you're starting your final year in a couple of weeks' time . . .'

Final year. I don't know how this is going to work. I can't go home. I can't. I can't.

'Are you okay, Sharon?'

I look to the left and to the right. I can stay here and work with Julia. I'll defer final year.

'Yes.'

'Oh, that sounds like Olivia.'

It is.

Julia explains that she'll write a report later and fax it to Olivia this afternoon, ready for me to take to my own doctor. At home.

'I can't go home.'

'Sharon, you can't stay here. You're not well and I can't leave you on your own. You can't come to work with me every day either. And whether you go back to do finals or not, you're going to have to go home eventually anyway. Let's get it sorted properly, as Julia says.'

'I'll make sure to explain things in my report. You won't have to say too much to your doctor.'

The room goes out of focus.

Home. Medical school. My doctor. Finals. Depression. Depression? Depression.

What is depression?

Most of us have felt down at times. We know what it is to be sad and miserable, but in depression these feelings persist for weeks or months, and they interfere with everyday life.

According to the Royal College of Psychiatrists in the UK, someone has depression if he or she has at least five of the following symptoms:

- Low mood, with persistent feelings of sadness, often worse in the mornings
- Tearfulness
- Fatigue
- Loss of appetite and weight (though some people eat for comfort and gain weight instead)
- Problems getting to sleep, then waking too early
- Reduced enjoyment in things they enjoyed previously (work, hobbies, interests, sex)
- Inability to cope with things as they used to, such as small changes in routine
- Loss of self-confidence
- Avoidance of other people

- Restlessness, irritability and agitation
- General loss of interest in life
- Feeling useless, inadequate and hopeless
- Having thoughts of suicide

These persist for weeks or months, and they are severe enough to interfere with everyday life.[1] Depending on the number of symptoms present, and their severity, depression is normally characterized as mild, moderate or severe.

Two days after arriving home from California, I attend my GP surgery. The duty doctor is a lady and I've never seen her before. I tell her that I have been to see a psychotherapist while staying with my aunt in California and that she thinks I'm not very well (I can't bring myself to say the 'd' word). I hand her Julia's letter and a tear runs down my cheek as she reads it in silence.

The doctor places the letter on the table, folds her hands and begins to ask me the same questions Julia asked. Yes, my mood is low. Yes, I have lost enjoyment in things. Yes, I am struggling to concentrate . . . struggling to sleep . . . struggling to eat. Yes, I have thought about suicide. But, no, I have no active intent.

I start to sob. This is pretty huge. I'm sick. I'm desolate. And I'm about to go back to medical school.

Flatly, her face quite hard, the GP declares that she agrees with Julia: I am depressed. Her assessment at this stage is that I am moderately depressed. She tells me that she would not usually prescribe medication immediately, but since I am at a critical point in my career, she is going to give me an antidepressant and refer me to a psychiatrist on an urgent basis.

'Can I see a therapist?'

'I'm not sure that there's provision for that. Let's see what the psychiatrist says, okay?'

That's it. I have a formal diagnosis, and there's not going to be a 'Julia' to talk it through with. The thought of seeing an actual psychiatrist terrifies me. I know I've been taught by psychiatrists, but to be referred as a patient is something else altogether.

I walk away, prescription in hand – a prescription that I am too ashamed to hand to my regular pharmacist. This is not migraine medication. I divert to a chemist's a mile away where no one knows my face.

What are antidepressants and when are they helpful?

Antidepressants are drugs that affect the concentration of two chemicals found in the brain – serotonin and noradrenaline. These are 'neurotransmitters' which convey messages from one brain cell to another and are thought to be involved in changes in mood.[2]

In mild depression, changes in behaviour (such as taking more regular exercise or connecting more with other people) and talking therapies (such as cognitive behavioural therapy) have a greater impact on mood than drugs. Antidepressants are needed when depression is more severe or persistent. It is usually two to three weeks before the effects start to be noticed and they should be taken for several months after the mood improves. If someone has repeated episodes of depression, they may be advised to take antidepressants on a long-term basis.[3]

Even in severe depression, most psychiatrists believe that antidepressants are most effective when they are used side by side with talking therapy. Talking therapy can address thought patterns and behaviours that may be perpetuating the depression, and helps people to understand some of the aspects of their life and history that have contributed to the development of the illness.[4]

Shame. It's as though the shame of depression affects me almost as much as the illness itself. I feel as though having depression means that there is a fatal flaw at the very core of my inmost being. I am too ashamed to be a friend with depression: I don't even tell my flatmate. Instead, I hide my antidepressant packet in my personal food cupboard and pretend that everything is 'just fine'. I am too ashamed to be a medical student with depression: I tell none of my classmates. I am too ashamed to be a Christian with depression: I tell no one at church.

I don't think much about God. He doesn't seem relevant now. I'm not angry with him, but I don't cry out to him either; I am too numb to pray at all.

I keep going to church on Sundays, but I stop playing my flute in the Praise Group. Final year has to be my priority, doesn't it? I know that, back in LA, my aunt and uncle are praying for me, but that's about as much pastoral support as I want.

I begin to use the excuse of medical school as a means of cutting everything – and everyone – else out. Once my placement begins, I arrive at the surgical unit in time for the 8 am ward round and I stay late into the evening, sometimes hanging around the Accident and Emergency Department seeing patients until after midnight.

I am a model student – one doctor, having seen me diagnose a case from an indistinct X-ray film, calls me the 'best final-year in the hospital' – but I am a faltering human being.

The first couple of weeks of my attachment complete, I brace myself for my first appointment with a psychiatrist. Can he or she rescue my medical career? Can he or she rescue me?

2

The symphonies have lost their colour
Wrestling with low mood

I steady myself on a railing as I arrive at the Royal. I take a few steps in the direction of the wards, then turn. I want coffee. I need coffee. I haven't slept, and I can't think. My mind is a black cave filled with stagnant water and glutinous sludge.

The drink is hot, but I don't feel my mouth burning. I walk into the elevator that serves the surgical unit and lean against the side wall. I can see myself in the mirrored walls. I look terrible. Dark, vacant eyes, sallow cheeks, dry lips. I try to smile and my face looks like a five-year-old has put it together from pieces of three different jigsaws. And my trousers. I've put an extra hole in my belt and now the excess material is pleated together at the front. I'm one of the last generation of medical students to wear white coats and I vow to put mine on as soon as I reach the ward.

On the sixth floor, I stop for the tiniest millisecond to consider the open fire escape . . . Sharon, you can't think like that. No. Just no. Wait for this afternoon, at least. See what the doctor says.

I join two classmates in the tutorial room. There's a note scribbled for us on the whiteboard: 'Assess Mrs Brown – meeting to discuss her case at 2 pm.' Mr Foster, one of the surgeons, is supposed to teach us then, but I won't be there. I make a mental note to call his secretary and tell her that I have a medical appointment. Medical.

Much more acceptable than saying I am going to the Department of Psychiatry.

James and Emma saw Mrs Brown yesterday, so they head to the Accident and Emergency Department. They both still need to get their arterial blood gas testing signed off, and I assure them – having spent long hours there – that A&E is the place where they'll get a chance to do it.

Mrs Brown is a little confused, but pleasantly so, and still capable of giving a history. I launch into the usual questions.

'Tell me about your pain . . . When did it start? . . . Where is it? . . . Does it spread anywhere else? . . . How would you describe it – is it sharp or dull? . . . Is the pain constant or does it come and go? . . . Does anything make it worse? . . . Does anything make it better?'

I lose my train of thought and find myself distracted by the clouds outside the window.

'Sorry, Mrs Brown. You've been very helpful. Now, do you mind if I put my hand on your tummy?'

I have her lie flat and expose her swollen belly.

'Aarrghh!'

I withdraw my palm. 'So sorry. Is that sore?'

'No! Your hand's freezing!'

It's like all my circulation is going to my brain, trying to keep it conscious . . . trying to keep it alive.

'I'm so sorry.'

I rub my fingers together vigorously and try again.

'Is that better?'

'Yes. Thank you.'

After I have examined Mrs Brown, I trudge once more to the cafeteria, praying that no one I know will be there. It's only 10.15 so I'm hoping none of the ward rounds have finished yet. It seems that they haven't. The only person I recognize is an elderly man I examined last week, obvious because of his double amputation. He's drinking tea and fingering a cigarette. Hospital campuses are not smoke-free zones yet, but he'll have to wait until he gets outside.

My Americano drained dry, I brace myself for returning to the ward. I think about whether I should give up and go home to bed, or if that will just make the wait worse. I wonder what it's like going to a psychiatrist. Will it be a man or a woman? My letter just says 'Dr Benjamin, Consultant', and I didn't do my psychiatry placement in Belfast – thankfully (how embarrassing that would be) – so I don't know the staff. My hands tremble and my legs feel weak, even though I'm sitting down. I should probably eat something, but I have no appetite. I pick up my *Oxford Handbook of Clinical Medicine* and move on. For now, at least, I'm not a patient.

Upstairs, a junior doctor grabs me.

'Sharon, go and see Mr Stubbs. His X-ray's really impressive.'

I don't feel that anything will impress me right now, but I stumble towards Room 4 anyway.

'Take some deep breaths for me, nice and slow.'

I move my stethoscope from side to side across his broad back, comparing 'like with like'. There are definitely bronchial breath sounds – where it sounds like you're listening over the windpipe instead of the tiny airways of the lower lungs – at the base of his chest on the right, with crackles throughout both lower lobes. A pneumonia?

The X-ray is 'impressive', even if it hurts my eyes to look at it against the lightbox. Not just pneumonia, but a significant tumour underlying the infection.

The junior doctor finds me standing in the corridor.

'What do you think?'

I want to cry, not because of Mr Stubbs' diagnosis, but because I wish it was my own instead. I take stock for a second. I do need help, don't I?

Somehow, I get through the morning. I leave the unit at one o'clock to get to my two o'clock appointment in good time. There's a bus from one hospital to the other, but I want to walk. I find the rhythm of putting one foot in front of the other mildly therapeutic, or perhaps it's just that exercise releases endorphins. Either way, it's better than being in close proximity to other people, and I feel as though there's an arrow pointing to my head with the word 'mental' written on it.

* * *

As I walk up the path towards the building that houses the Psychiatry Department, my knees literally knock together. I can hear them. I try to keep my breathing measured, but I can't control my racing heart.

I go through the double doors, appointment letter in hand, and look for Reception. There doesn't seem to be one. Then I hear a voice calling me from the left.

'Hello, are you okay?'

A man is sitting in a booth with a reinforced-glass screen in front of him. He looks like a bank teller. I shuffle over and push my letter through the slot at the bottom of the screen.

'Okay, you're here to see Dr Benjamin. I think it will be Dr Phipps, his senior registrar, today. Take a seat and he'll be with you soon.'

Oh. I am disappointed. I thought somehow that, as a final-year medical student, I would be passported straight to the top doctor.

What exactly is a psychiatrist?

A psychiatrist is a medical doctor with a primary degree in medicine and surgery, and several years of postgraduate experience in the practice of treating both physical and mental disorders. The psychiatrist uses many of the same skills that the physician uses to assess and treat a patient:

- Taking a history (and often a collateral history from someone close to the patient, which can be more important than in physical medicine)
- Observation of the patient (including appearance, tone of voice and behaviour)

- Using appropriate investigations (often to exclude physical causes for disease)
- Arriving at a diagnosis
- Evaluating and discussing treatment options
- Prescribing medicines and other treatments
- Assessing the effectiveness of a disease management plan over time, in collaboration with other members of the multidisciplinary team that he or she leads

It is worth remembering that the Bible validates the role of doctors and of medicine:

> Jesus said, 'It is not the healthy who need a doctor, but those who are ill.'
> (Matthew 9:12)

Jesus had powers to deliver people from disease, and they far exceeded those of medical practitioners, but still he recognized that sick people benefited from the expertise of those who had devoted their lives to learning about illness and how to treat it. Psychiatrists, in short, are expert doctors who tend to the sick in mind.

I take a seat in the back row. The waiting room has no windows and smells of stale coffee and body odour. There is a TV on a bracket near the door playing one of those early-afternoon soap operas, but I don't think anyone is watching it. The noise irritates my head, which is already sore.

Four others are waiting. To my right is a man dressed in a business suit, jotting notes in a diary. I don't know whether he is a patient or a drugs rep. He looks too well to be depressed, or anxious, or psychotic, but who knows? Maybe he has OCD or something . . . or maybe he has just got better . . . if that happens.

Standing beside the vending machine is an old-before-his-time man – perhaps in his forties, but wrinkled and nicotine stained – in a scruffy shirt and baggy jeans. He shifts his weight from one foot to the other and his expression is blank. He tells the receptionist he is just going 'for a ciggy' and steps outside the door.

In the front row, a couple sit together, she in bohemian dress, he in motorbike leathers. I don't know which one is the patient. They both look a little unusual, but she seems the more agitated, whispering something I can't hear in his ear several times and running her hand through her purplish hair.

A door behind me clicks open and a man of about my age – another university student, perhaps – walks out past me. He is bent forward as if he has osteoporosis, but I judge from his facial expression that he just has the weight of the world on his shoulders.

What do I look like, I wonder? Dressed in black, carrying a heavy bag full of textbooks, probably a bit unkempt. I am shaking. Fear is close to overwhelming me. Yet I could be on the verge of getting help. Could be.

The door behind me opens again and this time a curly head peers around the partition and calls me.

'Sharon? Ah, Sharon. Just follow me this way.'

He opens a door behind the partition using a numbered code and we enter a rabbit warren of blue-painted corridors. It's dark and the floor is dirty. It couldn't be more different from Julia's leafy courtyard in LA.

He walks quickly but looks round to check that I am still behind him. I'm there all right, walking on jelly legs. Eventually, he opens a door and ushers me into an office. There are books and files on a shelving unit that fills three walls, and a pile of journals, topped by the latest *British Journal of Psychiatry*, sits in the corner.

He motions to a chair and I gladly sit down, facing him across a narrow desk. He gets out a filing pad and an expensive-looking pen. He looks quite debonair in his morning suit, but his face is kind.

'Well, Sharon. I'm Dr Phipps, Dr Benjamin's registrar. I think he's going to pop in later, but are you happy to talk to me first?'

I nod.

'Thank you. I can see you're anxious, but there's nothing to be afraid of. We'll just have a chat about some of the things that are troubling you, and then we'll see if there's anything we can do to help.'

I nod again.

'I hear you're a final-year medical student but you've been having some problems with your mood. Is that right?'

'Yes.'

'I see your GP has prescribed an antidepressant for you.'

I don't know if I'm going to be able to speak. My tongue is stuck to the roof of my mouth.

'Do you want to tell me about what's been happening – how you've been feeling?'

I look at my hands.

'Your GP thinks you are quite low.'

'Yes.'

Very low. So low that it suddenly seems pointless to be here. But Dr Phipps' expression is encouraging, and I push myself to tell him more.

'I feel sad all the time, for no reason. It's like I'm surrounded by blackness.'

'That sounds hard. Are you finding enjoyment in anything? What are your usual pastimes – outside of medicine?'

He's trying to connect with me. I find my speech loosen.

'I like music, normally, but it feels as though the symphonies have lost their colour. Every note sounds the same. I used to go to the Ulster Orchestra's concerts, but I guess I've lost interest.'

I don't mention playing flute and piano in the Praise Group. That seems irrelevant, from another lifetime.

'And what about your course – are you enjoying it?'

I feel defensive. I can't allow anything to get between me and my career.

'Yes. It's good.'

He takes a deep breath and I know he knows I'm lying.

'But what about your concentration, your motivation?'

I tell him that it's hard. That I'm fatigued. That I take ten coffee breaks a day just to get through. But I'm so highly motivated. I know that I'm an honours student and I'm determined to prove it.

He asks about my sleep and I tell him that it's disrupted, that I keep being visited by a figure in a white shroud and I'm not sure if I'm dreaming or not but I know it represents me.

He looks concerned for a second but then straightens and continues.

Appetite? I have none. It's hard to eat. And I don't feel like I deserve food.

'You look thin. Do you think you've lost weight?'

I have, but please don't focus in on this. It's a secondary problem.

'A little.'

'I think we'll get your weight before you leave. Just to keep an eye.'

We talk more. I start to feel comfortable in this incongruous setting and I open up about what is happening in those deep invaginations of my murky mind, where demons and darkness abound.

Finally, he gets to the crux of the interview.

'With all of this going on for you, do you ever feel like life is not worth living?'

He's almost writing it already, that acronym with which I became so familiar in my psychiatry placement: TLNWL – thoughts that life is not worth living. I nod again and watch as he notes it down in large letters.

'I see. And you know that I need to ask you this. Do you have any thoughts of suicide? Any plans to hurt yourself?'

I hesitate for a second. The fire escape. That extra packet of paracetamol in the medicine cabinet. Fleeting, fleeting thoughts; transient still, but definitely there.

'No plans.'

'You've had thoughts?'

'Yes, but not right now.'

He pauses, writes something more which I can't read from where I'm sitting. Typical doctor's scrawl.

He leans back in his chair, twiddles his posh pen.

'How do you think you are, Sharon? Do you think you are well?'

I shake my head.

'Well, I think you are very depressed – moderate or perhaps even severe depression. And I think we're going to have to see you regularly here. Sharon, I think you need to think about taking a break from medical school . . .'

No! No way! That is the one thing that no one can take away from me. I know I will die if I can't keep up my placements. Days with nothing to fill them but my shadowy thoughts? I'd go mad. And what would I be if I wasn't a medical student? I'd be nothing. There'd be nothing of me left. Medicine is my identity . . . my purpose . . . makes my meagre existence worthwhile. Kind of. It's my survival strategy. It gives me a sense of control. I can't let go.

He reads my expression.

'You look like you don't want to give up yet.'

'I can't. I need to . . . I need distraction.'

'Hmm. I do understand that that's important too, but it's an awfully arduous way to distract yourself. I've been in final year and I know the strain that it puts you under.'

There's a knock on the door. Phew! I want this discussion to end.

Another curly head looks around the door and steps in.

'Oh, Sharon. Meet Dr Benjamin. He'll be in charge of your care and . . . I think . . . he'll want to see you soon too.'

'Hello, Sharon. Good to meet you.'

'Hello.'

'We're nearly finished here. Did you want anything?'

'No, just to introduce myself. I'll leave you to it, but any questions and I'm next door.'

He gives a little wave and reverses back out again.

'Now, where was I? Yes, I think we do need to let your clinical tutor know – the one responsible for your welfare.'

I shake my head. I can't have them know in uni. Shame . . . again.

'Sharon, you're going to need time off to come here, and I think you'll need some flexibility with your studies for a while. I think someone has to know. If I do a letter, will you take it to them? Or would you prefer me to send an email if you give me the address?'

The email, definitely.

'Okay. We'll have to leave it there. You look exhausted. Do you have any questions?'

I don't.

'Then just come with me to the clinical room and we'll get your weight and your blood pressure.'

I feel a sense of dread overcome me. I stand up and fall back into my chair again. I steady myself on the desk as I get up a second time.

'Maybe your blood pressure is low.'

But it's not. My weight is, though, but Dr Phipps doesn't comment.

'Okay, that's that then. Come with me and I'll let you out, and you can ask Terry in Reception for a two-week review. He'll give you a card. Oh, and here's a note for your GP – I think we'll increase your medication a little.'

He keys in the code again and shows me through the door to the waiting room.

I have to queue for Terry as the couple from the front row earlier are speaking to him ahead of me. As I stand there, I feel a sudden tap on my shoulder, waking me from a weary reverie. It's Dr Phipps. He shows me a clipboard with numbers on it. As an after-thought, he has calculated my body mass index. It's 16.7. Low. Like, technically anorexic low. He draws a big circle around it with his red pen and looks at me.

'I want to see that up next time. Please look after yourself.'

I am struck again by the genuineness of his expression. I realize that I am glad to have come. Still, I burrow my face into my scarf as I leave. I don't want anyone to spy me anywhere near here. Home, quickly, home.

* * *

The first term of final year continues in a similarly excruciating vein.

Each day I see patients, carry out procedures – heart traces, venous cannulations, suturing – prepare for tutorials (and work very hard to stay upright during tutorials), go to theatre with the surgeons, study in the library, drink a lot of coffee and wrestle with my thoughts.

And every Monday I go to the Department of Psychiatry.

At first, I continue to see Dr Phipps, but he grows more and more concerned about me. He asks Dr Benjamin to play a greater role. Eventually, Dr Phipps steps back altogether. My antidepressant dose is raised and raised again, but my thinking grows darker and darker, my mood drops lower . . . and my weight drops with it.

I am now diagnosed with major depressive disorder and 'eating disorder not otherwise specified' (EDNOS), because I meet the weight criterion for anorexia nervosa but do not seem to have the disturbed body image or fear of fat which are pronounced in most eating disorders. I realize that my illness is becoming more and more visible to those around me, but I keep shrugging off even the sincerest enquiries after my health. 'I suppose everyone is a bit overworked at the moment, but I'm fine, thanks.'

What is EDNOS/OSFED?

I was diagnosed with EDNOS in 2006, but this term is no longer used: psychiatrists now prefer 'other specified feeding or eating disorder' (OSFED) where symptoms do not fit the classic diagnostic criteria for anorexia, bulimia or binge-eating disorder.[1] Psychiatrists recognize that OSFED can be just as serious as other eating disorders and that it often endangers physical health.[2]

I shivered with cold and developed downy hair on my arms; my heart rate slowed and my blood pressure dropped; my periods stopped; I was diagnosed with osteoporosis, caused by hormonal disturbances associated with weight loss. I could have died from the physical complications of my eating disorder even if I had not suffered from other mental illness as well.

I knew that I was thin, but I did not feel that I deserved food, and I discovered that the high that resulted from starvation numbed my feelings of depression.

Again and again, the psychiatrists suggest that I take time off – even just two weeks in the first instance – and they offer to ensure that I am excused from tutorials. I am now struggling to enunciate any kind of answer to questions in the same tutorial groups where I was excelling at the start of term, but still I refuse. As I said earlier, I am dependent on my medical degree for my meaning, my identity, my worth and my sense that I control something on this earth. I know that if I stop going to my placements, everything will fall apart.

I still attend church, though less regularly – there are learning opportunities to be had on the wards at weekends too (so we keep being told) – but church doesn't mean very much to me or have any impact on my behaviour or thought patterns. I know somewhere deep down that I am finding my feeble security in the wrong places, but I don't really admit this to myself: letting go is too frightening. I stop praying, stop playing worship music, stop engaging with Christian friends; I can't muster the energy or interest to read the Bible. My faith is effectively dormant.

My doctors aren't anti-God or anti-Christianity, but they never mention matters of religion. During my career, I can remember hearing doctors (including psychiatrists) ask patients questions such as, 'Do you have a faith that helps you in times like these?' or, 'Is there anything that keeps you going when life is hard?' But my own psychiatrists do not ask me about my beliefs. Probably because I never tell them that I am a Christian. I even start to ask myself whether I still want to be a Christian – whether there's any point.

Christmas comes and goes, and things are only getting worse. I am barely functional and my body is starting to fail me. I have to attend for regular heart tracings myself because my pulse is so slow, and my blood pressure has dropped in tandem with my weight. I am shutting down, closing myself off. I won't let God save me. I can't save myself. I have written finals looming in January . . . and I am dying.

Can anyone – anything – rescue me now?

3
'I want to go home'
Wrestling with my loss of freedom

It's a Thursday in late January and I've just finished my written final exams – several two-hour papers asking me about everything from Huntington's disease to fragile X syndrome and the Krebs cycle. I'm exhausted and cold and relieved and depressed, but quietly confident that I've done enough to pass.

I have to see Dr Benjamin in the afternoon. He wants to know how I've got on.

'Hello, Sharon.'

'Hello.'

'Well, finals all over?'

'Until the clinicals.'

'Of course. You've done well to get this far, but I think we have to look at where we're at now.'

His expression is very earnest.

'Sharon, this isn't going the right way. I can't watch you go down any lower. It wouldn't be right. I'd be neglecting my duty of care to you.'

His eyes meet mine for a second.

'Are you still having thoughts that life is not worth living?'

'Sometimes.'

'And you're not well physically. Your clothes are hanging off you and your lips are blue.'

It's true. If I was having trouble walking to class before the exams, I'm struggling to find the energy to brush my teeth now.

'I think we need to admit you to hospital.'

But hospital? I push my chair backwards and sit up straight. That's not an option.

He continues.

'There's a bed upstairs. I want you to come in today.'

'I can't . . .'

'Why not, Sharon?'

'I don't want . . . I couldn't tell anyone . . . I'm, I'm . . .'

Shame. Fear.

'Sharon, I'm telling you that you at least need a rest – some support. There'll be nurses there for you 24/7. How about agreeing on a few days? Aren't you free for a week or so now anyway?'

It's true. I need a rest and there are no classes for ten days. But that doesn't mean I'm ready to go into hospital.

'Listen, you go home and pack some things for a couple of nights and I'll arrange for a taxi to collect you in an hour or so.'

He's deadly serious. I don't have any words. I haven't even come to terms with being a psychiatric outpatient and he wants me to be an inpatient. I don't know why, but it has never really occurred to me that this could happen – even with my increasingly frequent admissions of suicidal thoughts . . . or the decreasing numbers on the scales.

'But . . .'

'No buts. I'll see you in the ward later. They're kind up there. It's the best thing for you – honestly.'

I walk home like an automaton and pack my bags – just a few things since I won't be staying long – and hope that my housemate doesn't get home before the taxi comes. I'm just going to disappear. Maybe I'll tell her something tomorrow. Maybe not.

* * *

I arrive back at the hospital. There are two doors leading to the ward, one to either side of my usual entrance to the outpatient department. One has a laminated A4 page saying 'Female' stuck inside the reinforced-glass window. This is where I am to present myself. My steps are heavy as I slowly creak the door open and make my way up the rough-hewn stairs.

A nurse meets me at the top.

'You must be Sharon.'

I nod, speech failing me.

'Come this way. The doctor isn't ready for you yet, so you can wait here. I'll get you a cup of tea – how do you take it?'

She points me to a schoolroom chair against a wall at the junction between two corridors. I sit down, dropping my sports bag onto the floor beside me.

'Just a little milk, please.'

She smiles and walks away up the corridor which seems to link the female and male wards, and disappears into a room on the left.

I breathe in sharply, my head spinning for a second. This is really happening.

Patients move up and down the corridor and in and out of another room which I can't see. Cigarette smoke wafts from it every time the door opens. I choke a little.

Psychiatric patient. Those two words circle in my head endlessly. I am a psychiatric patient. My medical student identity seems to fade away. It's irrelevant here. I am no more a doctor than the girl lingering close by me with a frightened gaze and stains of breakfast and lunch down her ample front.

I have a 'Where are you, God?' moment, but I'm too numb to feel anger or resentment. I just feel distant from him . . . from everyone and everything. Separate. Detached. Corralled in a madhouse.

I adjust my position and my chair wobbles. Everything here is overused and worn. The walls, once pale green but now yellowed by smoke, have patches where the paint has peeled and the magnolia of years gone by shows through. The doorframe beside me is peeling too, and the navy carpet is threadbare and sticky from spills. This is a place that time forgot. I wonder how anyone gets better here . . . if anyone gets better here.

I resolve to tell the nurse that I'm going home. I'm going to be okay and I appreciate their help, but I don't belong here.

She seems to be taking some time.

Almost opposite me, a young woman with a nose ring and wearing a green uniform is sitting in a chair outside what looks to be a single room. Most of its furniture is in the corridor. Suicide watch? She smiles and waves at me, mouthing, 'You'll be okay.'

This makes me cry. I pull a crumpled tissue from my sleeve and wipe my face. My tears are hot.

A patient – a girl who can't be more than nineteen or twenty – walks past and stares at me for a moment. She has fiery red hair and a pale face. She continues on, stopping every few seconds to look up and to the left at something which neither I nor anyone else can see.

Then a broad-shouldered woman of around forty passes me in the other direction, turns and starts to pace up and down the corridor that connects the two wards. She's talking to herself and making wild gestures, and she smells of weed.

I notice a man coming out of the smoking room. He walks towards me. His shirt is hanging out and his fly is undone, and his long hair can't have been washed in weeks. I recoil as he stretches out a hand to shake mine.

'Edmund! Go back to your end and leave the young lady alone.'

I sigh out. The nurse has come back with my tea just in time.

'I hope that's all right for you. I'm not a tea-drinker myself, so I'm always guessing. I'm Jessica, by the way. I'll be your key nurse. Now, I'll bring your bag and we'll find your bed.'

I heard nothing after 'bed'. I clear my throat. My bed. Psychiatric patient, psychiatric patient, psychiatric patient . . .

Jessica shows me into a large space with a partition in the middle and nine beds around the edges, all facing towards the centre. She sets my things on the one closest to the door. A 'few days' – for a rest. No. No. I can't stay here.

'Can I speak to the doctor? I want to go home.'

'Well, the doctor isn't here at the minute, so why don't you stay here with me until he comes? It'll not be long.'

'I don't need to be here.'

I catch the eye of a plump, older lady sitting on a bed to my right. She gives a gentle, knowing smile and I try to smile back through my tears, managing only to lift the corners of my mouth into a grimace.

'Let's go through your stuff. I have to check for anything we need to keep for you.'

I push my wet hair out of my face, open my bag wide and pour out the contents of my little I'm-a-medical-student handbag, which include the *Oxford Handbook of Clinical Medicine* and a pen torch, on to the bed. Jessica confiscates a glass nail polish bottle and my razor.

'Okay, you can put the rest of your stuff in this cupboard. Do you want to finish your tea and I'll go and get your admission paperwork?'

My lips are parched but I haven't been able to swallow yet. The tea is lukewarm anyway.

Jessica disappears, and I look around me.

Opposite, someone has the curtains drawn around her bed and is playing rave music. The fabric billows and the curtains part. It's a blonde girl and she's dancing, a little offbeat, as if in a trance.

To the left, a middle-aged woman lies on her bed like a corpse, sheets pulled up so that only her eyes and dark hair are visible.

Another nurse walks in, uniform rustling.

'Betty, would you like some "time"?'

It seems that the plump lady on the right is Betty. She gets up to have whatever 'time' is.

I can hear male voices shouting in the distance.

The woman who smells of weed comes in and plops flat on the bed beside mine. I pull my curtains around me. I feel sick.

Jessica comes back with a wad of paper.

'Let's take this to the interview room where we'll have a bit of privacy. I'll just get your observations – your blood pressure and your height and weight – in the clinical room on the way. Is that okay?'

I don't suppose I have a choice.

'Mm-hmm.'

* * *

'I want to go home.'

Dr Benjamin said 'a few days'; it's been a week.

'You're not well. We need you to stay.'

The trainee doctor's face is set. There's a deep vertical crease between her eyebrows.

'But my placement starts on Monday.'

She sets down her pen.

'Sharon, you know you can't do your placement. You're too frail. And you can't stop crying. You've just told me about those dark thoughts. Placement can wait . . . Finals can wait.'

I recognize that what I'm saying sounds absurd. I want to die. I want to do my finals.

But to me the two are not mutually exclusive. I might put off dying until after I've done my finals. Yet I must graduate. Then I won't just be Sharon the psychiatric patient, Sharon the depressive, Sharon with the eating disorder. I'll be Sharon the doctor, Sharon the honours student, Sharon the success. And it doesn't matter what happens to me after that. All the effort I have put into this course will have been justified. Medicine is my identity, the only reason that I might even continue living.

'Please. I want to go home.'

'Then I'm going to have to get forms.'

Forms. I know what that means. The downy hairs on the sides of my face stand on end.

I am told that I cannot leave until I have been assessed by my GP. I slink to my bed, pull my curtains around me and try to reassure myself again and again that Dr Fullerton will surely see my point of view.

An hour or two later, Jessica calls me. Dr Fullerton has arrived.

'Take a seat there and he'll call you in a minute.'

My GP is in the ward manager's office and I wait on a chair in the corridor outside. There is a poster on the wall opposite me. It details the number of patients who have self-harmed, acted violently or gone AWOL in each month during the past year. Quite a lot, it seems. And I can already guess who might have been involved.

I am rehearsing my speech for the doctor, but I forget it when he opens the door.

'Sharon, come on through.'

I go in and he motions me to sit down.

'I'm sorry to see you in these circumstances.'

I feel my cheeks redden. Dr Fullerton pulls at his beard. His kindly face betrays his discomfort. He doesn't enjoy this any more than I do. He tries to pull his office chair closer to me, but there isn't any room to manoeuvre it around the ward manager's bulky desk. The arrangement is so much more formal than his own easy consulting room, which is only about 600 metres away as the crow flies.

'Well, how are you?'

It's an awkward start. He has come to assess my suicide risk, after all.

I feel tears drip from my jaw.

'I want to go home. My placement starts on Monday.'

'You're in your final year, aren't you?'

'Yes, I just passed my written finals.'

I feel like this information must surely reassure him. What detainable patient can say that?

'So I hear. That's quite an achievement, considering . . . ahem . . .'

He pauses, takes a breath.

'Sharon, you've told the nurses about some pretty serious symptoms – sinister thoughts, thoughts that your life isn't worth living. I've seen your file, the pictures you've drawn since you've been here . . .'

The paradox. Death and finals, finals and death.

'Are you still having thoughts of ending your life?'

They flow, a steady stream through my consciousness. I shrug. Honest to a fault.

'Do you have any plans to harm yourself?'

I choke on my saliva. I can't answer him. I look up at the rows of folders on the shelves. 'Health and Safety', 'Safeguarding', 'Data Protection' . . . No inspiration there.

'Sharon, you know I can't let you go.'

He taps on the forms in front of him with his pen.

'Are you sure you won't stay voluntarily? It would be better for you.'

'No. Please no. I'll be okay. Honestly . . .'

'If I thought you were okay, I would let you go. But it's my job to assess you and I've known you for a while and this is the worst I've seen you. Look, even for your body weight I'd have to consider detaining you. Your life is at risk if you don't start eating again.'

I try to wipe tears from my eyes, but my one tissue is soggy. He has a packet in his pocket.

'Here.'

I take two and blow my nose. This isn't going well.

I send up an arrow prayer: 'God, let me go home.' It doesn't work. Dr Fullerton puts pen to paper.

'Look, I can stop now if you'll just agree to stay.'

'No, no, no! I'm not staying.'

'Then I have to sign the forms.'

He pauses for a second, but I am just crying and protesting and he realizes that he's not going to reason with me. The familiar prescription signature flows from his nib. It's done.

What does detention mean?

In the UK, patients can be kept in hospital against their will, according to the terms of the Mental Health (Northern Ireland) Order (1986) or – in England, Scotland and Wales – the Mental Health Act (1983). Patients are then 'detained' or 'sectioned' and must remain in hospital until their detention order is lifted by a doctor. For people to be detained, they must have a diagnosable mental illness and be at risk of harming themselves or others.

Detained patients can be treated against their will, but they also have certain rights, such as the right of appeal to a Mental Health Tribunal and the right to speak with an independent advocate. Those who have been detained may still have visitors and may be allowed to leave their ward for short periods of time if this is agreed by their psychiatrist.[1]

I push my seat back and it falls over, but I don't care. I open the door and run from the room, run down the corridor, run to the exit at the top of the stairs. I don't think about the alarm that's going off as I scramble down towards the rickety door at the bottom. I don't think about anything except escaping from this prison.

I run, I run, I run.

Past the pharmacy buildings, through the car park, towards the main road. I am light and I feel like I'm floating.

'Aarrghh!'

Two strong hands grab me from behind. A voice speaks into a walkie-talkie.

'We've got her.'

The two security men have a firm hold of me now, one on each arm. As we turn back towards the Psychiatry Department, Jessica and the ward manager, Jason, arrive, panting.

'Come on, Sharon. This isn't helpful. Are you going to come with us or do we need these guys to escort you back?'

I shake my head. I'm defeated. I'm detained. I'm despairing.

4

Throwing the bouquet
in the bin
Wrestling with my identity

Detained in February 2007, I have no choice but to settle into the hospital routine.

Begrudgingly, I inform the university that I will not be in attendance at my three remaining placements – placements designed to prepare me for the clinical finals I am still determined to take in May. On the phone, my voice cracks. I feel humiliated.

The unit is crumbling but fairly well organized. We have breakfast at eight, relaxation therapy for fifteen minutes at 9.30 am, tea and coffee at ten, occupational therapy (OT) from 10.30 am till noon, followed by lunch. In the afternoon there is tea and coffee at 1.30, occupational therapy again from 2 to 3.30 pm, tea and coffee and visiting from 3.30 to 4.30 pm, dinner at 5 pm, another visiting time from 6 to 8 pm, supper at nine and bed at ten. And there are various 'medication rounds' in between, though I find myself visiting the nurses' station and their trolley more often as my use of PRN (additional, as needed) medication increases.

It is comfortingly predictable, but I also find it terribly dreary. I follow the timetable like a robot, present in body, absent in spirit, spending all my morning and afternoon sessions in the OT room painting pictures of coffins, bleeding wrists and tear-filled eyes.

The medical team are glad to know that I am staying. They set about assessing me more intensively – I feel as though I am being watched by hawks – and adjust my treatment accordingly. My antidepressant is changed, and in time a second is added. I am started on tranquillizers to help control my increasing agitation, and eventually an antipsychotic is prescribed as well, partly because of my unusual thoughts and in part to quieten me and suppress my urges to run away.

Still I continue to deteriorate. I become more and more detached from life, obsessed with death and barely eating enough to feed my addled brain, never mind my skinny body.

Yet that ambition to take finals still burns somewhere deep within me. I pester the doctors until they make an agreement with me whereby I am permitted to attend one tutorial per week – the most important class where we are expected to hone our clinical skills with properly sick patients, examining and diagnosing. The privilege is granted and I am allocated to a tutorial group that meets in a building just 200 yards away from the Department of Psychiatry. I am to eat my nightly sandwich, leave the ward at 5.20 pm for the class at 5.30 pm and return by 7.15 pm. I am assured that if I do not reappear in time, Security will be sent to retrieve me.

I play by the rules and continue to go to this class for about two months, palpating for enlarged spleens, listening to regurgitating heart valves, identifying the signs of liver failure – until I realize that my classmates have worked out where I am coming from and I feel too ashamed to show my face again.

They have probably known for some time. When you tell one or two classmates, the chances are that they whisper the secret to one or two more. In any case, it is obvious by my tortured expression and waif-like figure. I am a ghost who leaves the psychiatry ward wearing a white coat and carrying a stethoscope, just like one of those other-worldly characters who inhabit my dreams and present as visions in my waking hours.

Medicine does fade in its importance over time. I live under a heavy cloud of depression, struggling to think through a soup of negativity and bizarre intrusive images, and growing faint and

32

dizzy from starvation. However, I can't let go of the hope of graduating as a doctor. I reason through smoke and fairground mirrors: I am still a medical student first and foremost. This gives me a sense of self beyond that of being a psychiatric patient, compulsorily institutionalized and surely doomed to die in darkness and despair.

It is arranged that other professionals will become involved in my care. A dietitian called Alana comes to see me weekly, encouraging me to eat two scoops of mashed potato at lunchtime instead of one (and to put butter on them), and prescribing high-calorie supplement drinks and puddings to help me to put on some weight.

I refuse them again and again, making excuse after excuse to the nurses – 'I'm not hungry . . . I'm nauseous . . . I feel too full . . . I don't like the taste . . .' – and when I do take a drink, I pour half of it down the sink. I have no concern about looking fat; I simply don't think that I deserve food. To me, self-nourishment is self-indulgence. And since I'm going to die anyway – I've become increasingly certain of this – it doesn't seem as though there is any point in investing in my physical health.

I am also assigned to a cognitive behavioural therapist, who comes from an outpatient service to see me on Tuesdays. She is a slim blonde, attractive but quietly spoken, and I warm to her. I even work hard at the exercises she gives me, but depression always wins out.

I write down a thought – 'I'm worthless' – and then I have to find evidence to support and dispute it, weighing up whether it's really true or not. I identify something to counter the thought – 'I'm a medical student and I've already passed my written finals' – but I write reams about why the thought is true: 'I am a failure. I got through four and a half years of medical school and still ended up on the scrapheap in a psychiatric hospital. I'm never going to be a doctor, so what was the point? A medical degree has no worth if you're never going to practise. My life is meaningless. I have no worth whatsoever.'

In the end, I reinforce my negative thinking so much that the therapist decides that further treatment is only going to be unhelpful. Her visits stop. Talking therapy can't help me. I must be a hopeless case. My despondency deepens.

What is cognitive behavioural therapy?

According to the Royal College of Psychiatrists, cognitive behavioural therapy (CBT) is 'a way of talking about how you think about yourself, the world and other people ... [and] ... how what you do affects your thoughts and feelings'.[1] It is a structured talking treatment in which people learn of how making cognitive changes (changes in how they think) and making changes in their behaviour affects how they feel. Rather than looking for the causes of someone's problems in their past, a CBT therapist will focus on finding solutions to the problems in the present. CBT is particularly useful in depressive disorders and in anxiety, but is also beneficial to those with other mental illnesses such as bipolar disorder and schizophrenia.[2]

Should a Christian have CBT?

The Bible often speaks of the importance of our thoughts, and I believe that the CBT approach is consistent with its teaching.

The New Testament includes a series of letters from a Christian leader called Paul to some of the churches that were founded as Christianity spread, to encourage the believers in the faith. He addressed the issue of managing thoughts when he wrote to the church at Corinth:

> We demolish arguments and every pretension that sets itself up against the knowledge of God, and we *take captive every thought* to make it obedient to Christ.
> (2 Corinthians 10:5, emphasis added)

In CBT, the goal is to transform destructive thought patterns and to create a healthier perspective, with consequent positive effects on behaviour and emotions. This aim is supported by the book of Romans, Paul's summary of Christian theology:

Do not conform to the pattern of this world, but *be transformed by the renewing of your mind*. Then you will be able to test and approve what God's will is – his good, pleasing and perfect will.

(Romans 12:2, emphasis added)

The Bible can be an additional tool for Christians who are undertaking CBT, as they can ask themselves, 'Do my depressed/anxious/disturbing thoughts line up with what Scripture says about me?'

Fellow Christians can support those who are engaged in CBT, validating that what they are doing is scriptural and helpful, praying for them and offering practical support (such as transport to appointments).

But there is one group of people who don't give up on me. Detained and hopeless, I decide to tell my pastor where I am. It just seems like the right thing to do, even if God has become an irrelevance. A steady stream of church visitors begins, and it continues to flow in spite of my lack of engagement. One senior pastor brings me the *Book of Common Prayer*, thinking that it will help me when I can't find words. I open it once or twice, but it soon ends up on top of my wardrobe. Similarly, a lady who practises Christian 'listening' arrives with pamphlets of simple liturgies and books by Henri Nouwen. I barely look at them.

But I do appreciate their presence. I know deep down that they really care about me, and that means something, even if I don't care about myself any more. And if nothing else, their visits are a welcome distraction from the tedium of ward life.

Months pass – February, March, April – and May is exam time. Although I have effectively dropped out of medical school, I contact the university and they are prepared to let me take finals. My obstacle is Dr Benjamin, who feels that I am by no means well enough to subject myself to that kind of stress. I protest forcefully, pleading my case: 'I've come this far and you're going to stop me from graduating?' 'I promise I'll take my supplements [high-calorie drinks] every day if you let me go . . . I'll have absolutely no reason left for living if you take this away from me.'

Ultimately, he concedes. 'I don't understand how you're going to do this, but I don't think you'll forgive me if I say no.'

So, on 15 May 2007, the ward doors are opened for me at 8 am. I don my white coat, get on the link bus for the Royal Hospital and arrive in the Day Procedure Unit, which has been closed in order to host the medical final exams. In the waiting area I stare at my spindly fingers, not wanting to catch anyone's eye. The other students are buried in their *Oxford Handbook* or flicking through flash cards anyway, but several throw me a sideways glance, surprised to see me and intrigued to know what I look like after so long in seclusion.

We have to assess eight patients in a series of OSCE – objective structured clinical examination – stations, and I am invited to begin at 9.30. At the bedside of my first patient stands an examiner whom I know well: he taught me frequently during my medical placement in the Royal at the beginning of my fifth year – the placement where I had been called 'the best final-year in the hospital'. His warm smile morphs into a wrinkled frown when he sees me. He shakes my feeble hand and holds it for a second, letting go slowly.

I am an object of pity.

The bell rings.

'Good morning, Sharon. Please assess the patient's cardiovascular system and identify her cardiac murmur.'

A simple enough exercise for an experienced medical student. But I blank.

Washing my hands as a matter of routine and to ground myself, I search my hazy brain for the schema which tells me what comes next.

I stare at the patient, and stare . . . and stare. He nods encouragingly.

'He-hello, Mr Hayes. My name is Sharon and I am a final-year medical student. Is it okay if I examine your chest?'

I'm getting somewhere, but I have missed examining the face, hands and ankles for signs of heart failure, and I have forgotten the all-important pulses.

I hesitate. The chest, the chest.

'Could you sit up and lean forward a little for me please. Yes. Now I'm just going to lift your shirt, if that's okay . . . Right, take deep breaths in and out through your nose. That's it. Thanks.'

I'm running out of time. The examiner looks perturbed.

I finish up and clasp my hands together.

'Er . . . have you diagnosed Mr Hayes's murmur?'

The murmur! The heart! I have performed a respiratory exam, and a cursory one at that. Aarrghh! I've flunked it. Now, what is the commonest murmur?

'Aortic stenosis.'

My answer is more of a question.

Mr Hayes looks down. He knows I'm wrong. The examiner shifts his weight to one foot.

'It's regurgitation, actually. I'm sorry.'

He writes something on his card.

The bell rings and I avoid his eye as I leave for the next station.

I've failed. I'm convinced of it.

But it's oddly reassuring. All those negative beliefs I have about myself – they're true.

I move through the remaining tests more smoothly. I'm aware that I'm missing things, and I'm close to passing out at times from hunger and hyperventilation, but I make no more gross errors. By the time I have finished, I wonder whether I might not actually have, on balance, passed after all.

Two days later, I get my result: it is a pass – only just (none of the once-predicted honours), but a pass nonetheless. A large bunch of flowers with accompanying balloons arrives at the ward. I burst the balloons and put the lovely fresh bouquet straight into the bin. All of the meaning that I had attached to passing finals has suddenly dissipated. I'm Dr McConville now. But for what? I have no job to go to – I haven't even applied – and I am a basket case, still detained, now destined for a specialist eating disorder unit in London.

Thoughts of suicide begin to dominate.

I don't want to see visitors; I don't want to speak to my treatment team. And I definitely don't want to hear about God. I feel abandoned, my situation irredeemable. Surely no one can help me now. I don't even want help; I just long for death. Death means darkness, an end to everything. All my hopes of heaven have been annihilated. I don't question God's existence, but I'm convinced that I am now separate from all of that 'Christian experience'. I will return to the ground, rot and be forgotten. I walk around like I'm a zombie already – waiting, waiting, waiting for the moment when I can escape and end it all.

5

A case too complex to treat
Wrestling with rejection

I look through my narrow window at the lawn and cultivated beds below. Two young women on their fifteen-minute 'walk' are powering along a winding path. I push my chair back from my tiny desk and it hits the bed: the room to which I am so often confined is a shoebox.

I hear movement next door. Lynn must have dropped something. Others are moving about. It's 1.48 pm. Almost time for group therapy, which is supposed to be our weekly opportunity to say how we're feeling and to gain support from others. Last week we all sat in silence. What a waste.

It's my third week in the EDU (the Eating Disorder Unit). I have gained some weight, and my hopelessness is a little less profound. I'm in London now, after all – there is real expertise here. The study outcomes are good. I've read them for myself.

I walk down the corridor, past a double bedroom. The door is open but I can see a curtain around Lucy's bed. Thud, thud, thud. She's doing star jumps. Again.

The meeting is held in a room that is almost entirely yellow – yellow carpet, yellow walls, yellow chair-cushions – it's almost like sitting in the trumpet of a daffodil. We form a circle and Angela asks who would like to begin. No one speaks for a full twenty minutes. Aside from the occasional sigh or the noise of Cynthia cracking her toe knuckles inside her ballet shoes, the gathering is silent.

Someone clears her throat. A tiny Eastern European girl called Zofia is about to speak.

'I feel sad.'

No one replies. Anna, her friend, who is sitting beside her, strokes her shoulder.

'No physical touch, please, ladies.'

Anna recoils and looks as though she is about to cry. The silence becomes even more awkward.

After another five minutes, Natalie sits up straight and coughs a little. She is a tall girl of slight build with pointed gel nails and just-so make-up.

'I was over my band again. Someone is still making my coffee with one-half milk; I'm supposed to have black coffee now. I'm on "harm reduction", aren't I?'

Natalie's eyes glint in the artificial light.

All of my communication skills training is surfacing. I am itching to defuse some of that emotion! Someone has to make these frustrating sessions more useful.

'You seem angry, Natalie. Would you like to tell us about it?'

Natalie snorts. The veins in her neck bulge.

'No . . . *doctor*. I would not.'

She spits out the word 'doctor' as if it's extra milk in her coffee. Her two sidekicks, Parminder and Grace, seated to her left and right, glare at me.

I feel my cheeks getting hot. Angela chooses to say nothing. In fact, no one says anything until three o'clock comes round and Angela gets up, signifying the end of the group.

Doctor. Doctor . . . doctor. The title I worked so hard for, used as an insult.

Later, I am sitting on my own in the common room, waiting for the evening snack, half awake, half dreaming, feeling tired and bored. There is so much empty space like this when there could be some kind of therapy. I keep telling myself that it has to be this way, that we need time to think and process things, but the days are long and lonely . . .

'She's here.'

It's Parminder's voice calling out.

Two more bodies rustle in. It's Natalie and Grace. Suddenly, I am surrounded, Natalie leaning over me, her nose millimetres from my own; Parminder and Grace each leaning on an arm of my chair.

'Well, well. It's the "doctor". You think you're better than all of us, don't you? But you're not. You're worse. You're just a little anorexic who'll never be a doctor. Never. So just you keep your mouth shut in future and don't try giving us therapy.'

I sink backwards.

'Understood?'

I gasp. Are they for real?

If there's any doubt, they prove it the next day. I am cut out of the conversation at breakfast, and when I come into the art room, Parminder, who shares my desk, sits with her back to me. Then at snack time, Grace knocks my arm and I drop my biscuits.

'Looks like someone's trying to restrict, doesn't it?' Natalie's voice rasps. She walks away from me and tosses her coiffed hair.

The next day, the girls have their monthly election for the Weekend Activities Committee. I am the only person willing to stand who doesn't get a single vote.

'Sorry,' Lynn, my neighbour, who has been a sort of friend since I've been here, whispers. She gives a meaningful look in the direction of the three partners in crime, who have all been nominated. Is everyone under Natalie's thumb?

A week later, things are only getting worse. I meet with my individual therapist. We have said little to each other so far: his is the Freudian 'blank-canvas' approach, and I don't know how to begin, but today I have an agenda.

'I want to go home.'

He stops, takes off his glasses and decides to respond for once.

'Sharon, we all know you're unhappy. The staff aren't blind, you realize.'

Natalie. Parminder. Grace. They know, then.

'But you're not doing anything about them!'

'Anything we would do might make it worse. Come now. Group interaction is all part of the treatment. You've been doing well.'

'Gaining weight, you mean? I know. That's the easy part. But my mood . . . My thoughts . . . They were better when I first came here. But now . . .'

'You are feeling hopeless again.'

'Not totally.'

I don't want to get sectioned again.

'But I know I can't get better here. It's not what I expected. No one connects with me. And now I'm an outcast even among the girls.'

I pause, inhaling and holding it.

'I'm going home. I know what I have to do now. I'll eat the heavy puddings. I'll take the digestive biscuits. But I'll do it on my own.'

There are more arguments with doctors, nurses and dietitians. But, in the end, an occupational therapist speaks up in support of my case. She thinks I can manage as an outpatient.

I find myself on a plane two days later, eyes brimming, jaw clenched. Going home, but to what? I'm not better. I don't have a medical job. I don't even have a home.

I spend a month in temporary accommodation, eating cheesecake, my sanity slowly disintegrating.

One night, I open a box set and put on the first episode, desperate for distraction. But I can't focus. The dialogue seems distorted – impossible to follow. I feel utterly alone, and there are dark pictures in my mind's eye. Bloody, horrifying pictures. I feel an urge to see blood in the real world – to ground myself with actual physical pain.

In a state of heightened consciousness, I go to the bathroom and retrieve a razor. Back on my bed, still half watching the DVD, I cut myself for the first time.

Two days later, I am readmitted to the psychiatric ward, no longer frighteningly thin, but with terrifying thoughts. I am depressed, and now my mind and behaviour are chaotic. I run away again and again; I pour scalding tea over my hands; my dressing gown belt is removed after I threaten to hang myself with it.

The healthcare team try to work with me, even as their patience is tested. My antidepressant is changed, I am put on the maximum dose of a sedative antipsychotic, and my PRN tranquillizers are prescribed regularly instead. I pace the corridors, I stop eating again, my weight falls steadily and my thoughts are sparse and black.

In time, I become so heavily medicated that I speak little, sleep a lot and can barely process basic information. My chaotic behaviour has settled, but for what? I am the living dead.

'Please help me, Dr Benjamin. Please.'

'Things are at a standstill here, Sharon. There's nothing more we can do for you. Honestly, would you consider going back to London? Your weight is low again – not as low as before, but you meet the EDU entrance criteria easily. You can have therapy there. You need real talking therapy, and we just can't offer that.'

'But . . .'

'I know you were bullied before, but months have passed. Those girls were nearing the end of their treatment, weren't they? It would be a fresh start. You asked for my help, didn't you? Well, this is what I'm suggesting.'

I decide to go. I realize that I want to go. I need to get out of this ward. I need to get out of Belfast. Perhaps this time I won't even come back home. I could stay in London, have outpatient therapy, build a new life . . .

In my tiny moments of lucidity, I start to feel the beginnings of hope.

＊ ＊ ＊

Back in London, nothing is as I expected. I cannot slot straight back into therapy; I am put 'on assessment', which means that I can see my individual psychotherapist – the 'blank canvas' guy to whom I had struggled to speak before – and attend a weekly craft session and a group called 'projective art'. All other classes and groups are closed to me. I must prove that I am ready for 'the programme'.

I am also shocked to see that a few of the girls – including Lynn – who were at target weight and nearing discharge when I left, are now back in an emaciated state. Their 'recovery' was short-lived, wasn't it?

In individual therapy, I try to express myself. I talk of my deep depression and the ghoulishness of my thoughts. In projective art, while the other girls draw pictures of a skinny girl looking at her fat reflection in a mirror, I draw demons and ghosts and open wounds and graves. In craft class, I twiddle my knitting needles, unable or unwilling to follow a pattern.

I eat all that is set in front of me. What is the point in resisting? I see girls sitting for hours over meals with nurses waiting for them to dissect and nibble their chicken nuggets. I see girls refuse and then lose privileges. I see girls run screaming from the clinical room on weigh-in mornings because they have gained 0.1 kg. This is not what my eating disorder is about: I feel guilty when I nourish myself, but somehow not when others nourish me.

Between times, I am not allowed to leave my room. All communication with the other girls is discouraged outside of the therapeutic setting, and – since I'm not allowed to attend most therapy – I feel very alone. Sedated and so depressed that I ache all over, I curl up on my narrow bed, waking only when I am called for meals and snacks. I don't even want my fifteen-minute walks.

My weigh-ins show a steady gain. I think I am conforming to expectations. But.

It's Wednesday morning and one of the orderlies knocks on my door and drops a letter onto my desk. I am sitting with my milky coffee and digestives, with a gardening programme on in the background (I have borrowed a TV from a girl who is on home leave). I don't open the envelope until it is time to return my mug and plate to the kitchen.

The letter is brief. It says that my assessment period, initially intended to be two weeks, is to be extended. I am 'not ready to commence the programme'. I am 'showing a lack of engagement'.

My numb brain processes the information slowly. I break. More of this solitary confinement? More of these endless hours on my own with only turbulent thoughts and traumatic memories for company?

No, no. I can't do it. They have to admit me to the programme. I ask for a meeting with my therapist, protest, but to no avail.

I cope for twenty-four hours and then I can cope no more. I ask to leave again.

'But you left before and had to come back.'

'But you're very unwell. What about these thoughts of suicide?'

There are objectors all around. On Thursday afternoon, I am sectioned. Again.

But on Friday morning there is a ward meeting and I am called to attend.

'Sharon, we have been considering your situation very carefully. We know that you are upset that your assessment was extended. We felt that you were too unwell to undergo the challenging therapy required for recovery.'

I nod, thinking they have changed their minds.

'As a team we have reached a further decision. You are suffering from more complex mental illness than many of the girls here. You know that you have problems beyond your anorexia nervosa. Because of this, we don't feel that the EDU is the right place for you at this time. The recovery programme is hard work and you are not fit for it. Do you understand?'

I do. They don't want me to be a 'failure' on their programme. It would affect the statistics.

'We do hope that your condition will improve at home. Perhaps the right timing will come for another admission here in the future . . . But Miriam will arrange for you to fly back to Belfast as soon as it is convenient. We wish you all the best.'

Home. What hope is there for me now?

* * *

Back in Northern Ireland, I find temporary accommodation in a new area, which means that I fall out of the catchment area for Dr Benjamin's team and have a new GP. Dr Langley says that she can't manage my complex prescription on her own: I get an urgent referral to Dr Whiteside, another new psychiatrist.

I have been living in constant crisis. Too thin to have focused treatment for major depressive disorder; too depressed to have specialized eating disorder treatment. And occasionally self-harming too.

The day of my psychiatry appointment dawns bright and sunny. I am nervous, not because this is a psychiatry appointment per se (I have got used to being a mental health patient), but because I am desperate for help and I want this Dr Whiteside to understand the urgency of my situation.

I arrive at her outpatient clinic and she calls me almost immediately. She is middle-aged and plump, but with a pinched face.

I go in and take a seat and she doesn't look up at me when she speaks.

'Sharon? I've read your notes. I don't know why you've been referred to me. You've had the offer of expert care and it seems you haven't engaged. I don't believe that I can help you, so I'm going to discharge you.'

Haven't engaged?!

I lift my chin and raise a hand to my brow. Tears run. You can't discharge me!

'But my GP said . . .'

'Your GP will understand that we have nothing to offer you.'

I lift my bag and swing it over my shoulder as I turn and stumble out of the door. I feel as if injustice has thumped me squarely in the face.

Alone. Abandoned and alone. Surely now I will die.

At home, I message a friend.

Her reply is unexpected.

'Would you like to come with me to church on Sunday?'

Church? Seriously?

I'm not going to worship a God who leaves me high and dry. I'm not going to worship a God who clearly hates me.

I clench my teeth. I believe in God and I believe that he is a God of other people. I believe that I live in a parallel reality to other

Christians. A bleak, blank space devoid of God's love or compassion. Evil attacks me at every corner. Demons lurk behind my shoulders.

I am not evil, but I hate God. There it is. I have thought it. And I'm going to say it aloud.

'I hate God.'

No one can hear me, but I don't care. I scream it now.

'I hate you, I hate you, I hate you, God.'

I text my friend back.

'No thanks. I don't feel like it.'

6

He wants me back
Wrestling with God

I sit at the computer desk beside the window. The sun is shining, but there are storm clouds gathering just within my view. I hear a low, distant rumble.

I spin my pen. I know that I cannot stay with my parents much longer, know that I am ill, know that I am not likely to live for long. In my head, I have set an ultimatum: if there is no sign of help arriving within the next two weeks, I will end it. I am not sure how – yet – but I am determined.

I browse the internet, entering search terms like 'treatment for depression and eating disorder', 'psychiatric rehabilitation' and 'counselling for suicidal thoughts'. So many problems, so few answers. There seems to be very little available in the UK outside the NHS. There's the Priory, but the cost is incredible, and there were girls at the Eating Disorder Unit in London who were unsuccessfully treated at the Priory anyway. It does not entice me.

Almost whimsically, I start to look at options in North America. I soon find that private 'behavioural health centres' abound in the States. The sheer number of hospitals and residential facilities that Google generates confuses and overwhelms me. I turn away from the screen for a second.

New Beginnings. I recall the name of a specialist treatment centre in Arizona which I had come across as a medical student. I once worked as a volunteer Student Support Officer and I remember a female student who had an eating disorder and OCD (obsessive-compulsive disorder). She was being failed by local health services and I had cast a wide net when looking for help for her – even as far as the USA. I requested leaflets from New Beginnings online, never thinking that I might one day want one for myself. I passed them on to her, but it didn't lead to much. Now this is about me. Really.

I hesitate, nibbling at my fingernails, then type the name into the search engine.

There it is: 'New Beginnings Ranch – Specialist Treatment Facility for Women and Adolescents with Eating Disorders and Associated Mental Health Conditions'. My hand shaking, I click on the link.

This is not for me. I could never afford it. They would never take someone with conditions as complicated as mine. My thoughts spin.

But I read the blurb:

At New Beginnings, we specialize in treating women and girls who have complex mental illnesses and problems with eating behavior. We recognize that eating disorders are a manifestation of deeper psychological problems which must be addressed, and almost always co-exist with some form of depressive illness, anxiety, self-injury, personality disorders, substance abuse problems or other mental disturbances. We have a reputation for being able to help those who have been through multiple treatment programs and suffered repeated relapse. Today, over 8,000 alumni of our center are leading healthy, fulfilling lives.

Complex illness. Co-existing conditions. Repeated relapses. They're basically describing me.

I brush my hair out of my eyes. My lips tingle and a shiver runs down my spine.

But no, it couldn't be possible. Get a grip, Sharon. This place is in America, for people with American health insurance. You don't even have health insurance here. You probably couldn't afford to stay for a week.

Our programs last 45 or 60 days, depending on body weight at admission.

I look down at my bony knees. I'm sure I would be in the sixty-day category. I search the site for costs, but there is no information; instead, I'm continually directed to 'speak to our finance department today – we will work with you to find a solution to match your financial situation'. It sounds too good to be true. They can hardly match the financial situation of somebody who is broke, or even who – like me – has saved their five-year student loan in the hope of buying a new car some day.

The website sucks me in, though. I spend an hour looking at pictures of cautious girls learning to groom horses; small therapy groups meeting under trees; smiling psychiatrists and dietitians; and happy, healthy-looking women who have successfully graduated from the programme. I read testimonies from GPs who have referred 'difficult cases' to New Beginnings, from parents who thought that their daughters would die before they were admitted there, and from successful career women – some of them therapists themselves – who were treated only a few years ago for anorexia, depression and suicidal thoughts. Is it possible? No, Sharon, be realistic.

But my hand hovers over my phone. It's the early afternoon. I could ring my aunt in California. She would know whether or not it's just a pipe dream. But she'll think I'm ridiculous, that I'm asking for her money, that I'm setting myself up to be dangerously disappointed.

'Sharon?'

'Yes, Olivia.'

'How are you?'

'Just the same.'

'At your wits' end?'

'Yes.'

'I'm sorry, sweetie. Did you go back to your GP?'

'Yes. She's going to keep prescribing the meds.'

'That's good, at least.'

'Olivia?'

'Yes, love?'

'I've been on this website. There's a treatment centre that might be able to help me. But it's in America.'

'Where?'

'In Arizona. New Beginnings. They treat eating disorders and all sorts of mental illness – the cases other centres can't help.'

'Wait. I've got my laptop in front of me. Let me look it up . . . Okay, got it. It's a Christian centre?'

I've been ignoring that. It can't be central to the treatment, surely.

'Uh-huh. I guess.'

'Have you called them?'

'Olivia, they'd never take me, would they? I'm sure it's for American women. And I don't have insurance . . .'

'How much does it cost?'

'It doesn't say. You have to talk to their financial coordinator. It says they can work with everyone to find a solution to suit, but that's probably just if you have an insurance provider . . .'

'Call them.'

'But . . .'

'Sharon, call them.'

'What should I say?'

'Just find out what they can do. We'll help you if we can.'

'You're serious?'

'Absolutely.'

'Okay.'

'Good. Listen, sorry, but I'm on call – I have to go. Let me know how you get on.'

'I will.'

I sit there for a moment. My heart is beating fast. I might as well call them now, get it over with before I chicken out.

On the other end of the phone is a lady called Sarah-Ann with a cheery voice who calls me 'hun' a lot. She explains that there are 'options' for young women who do not have insurance, including an alumni fund that sponsors those who could not otherwise afford to have treatment.

'Everyone needs to pay at least 25% of the cost of the programme. Otherwise they wouldn't feel ownership of it. That's our policy. But if you meet certain criteria, you might get help with the rest, hun.'

I answer some questions and we establish that – incredibly – I do meet whatever 'criteria' the alumni fund might stipulate.

'So, do you think you can get that 25% together, hun? Because we'd love to help you. We don't want anyone to miss out on the treatment they need on account of money.'

I don't know. There's the student loan . . . and Olivia. How am I going to ask Olivia for that amount? It seems huge to me.

'Can I talk to my aunt about it?'

'Of course you can, hun. I've got a file set up for you here with the agreement we've come to. If you want to come back to me later today or tomorrow, we'll see if we can't get you admitted.'

I talk to Olivia and immediately she offers a significant sum. Another family member agrees to match it. Together with my £9,000 student loan, we can make up the 25%. I can't feel my tongue in my mouth when I talk. The coloured patches on the curtain beside my computer dance.

I take a deep breath and call Sarah-Ann back.

'I can do it.'

'You can make the 25%? Why, that's wonderful. I knew you were just meant to come here! Well, then, I can put you straight through to the intake department if you like?'

This is all a bit too easy. And happening too quickly. Intake? Am I ready for this?

I don't know what else to do. I know that I have run out of options here. I agree.

A note on treatment abroad

I am unusual in having had treatment abroad (and, incidentally, New Beginnings, as I knew it, is no more, having reopened with an adjustment in focus and culture). Such treatment is not covered by the NHS for UK patients, so it is usually prohibitively expensive. It is necessary to obtain specific visas for travel associated with medical treatment, and it is not possible to access conventional travel insurance.

Treatment for mental illness in the UK is generally of a good standard, and it should not be necessary, if you live here, to go elsewhere for quality care.

'No. Nooo! Nooo-woah . . .'

'Sharon, Sharon.'

'Let me go!'

I am against the wall, facing into the living area of the ranch house to which I've been assigned. There is a nurse holding each of my arms gently but firmly.

'Where are you going to go, honey? You're in the middle of the desert, thousands of miles from home. Let us help you.'

'NO! I want to DIE!'

'Sharon, that's enough. Enough, okay? You're scaring the other girls.'

I hear faint sobs coming from the common room. There's a small face with wide-opened eyes peering around the door frame. It is enough. I slide down the wall and crumple into a heap on the floor, crying but no longer screaming.

'I want to go to my room.'

'You can't go to your room. This is social time. Here, take this tissue and wipe your face. Let's go and join the other girls.'

What can I do? Abbie, one of the nurses, takes my arm and leads me, heels dragging, into the common room.

There are two girls sitting on the floor, colouring pictures from a book. One of them, Toni, a slight girl with an LA Tigers T-shirt on, pushes her hair out of her eyes and looks up at me. She speaks quietly.

'Would you like to colour? You can share these pencils.'

I shake my head. Colouring is for four-year-olds, not adult women.

Two girls are playing Connect 4 at a table; a blonde lady who must be in her late forties is scribbling something in a journal; a couple of others are reading books. I can see them all sneaking surreptitious looks at me.

Abbie asks me if I would like a book from the library, pointing at some shelving in the corner. I look at the titles. *Hinds' Feet on High Places* by Hannah Hurnard. Brennan Manning's *The Ragamuffin Gospel. The Message. Intuitive Eating.* Christian books, self-help books.

'All of these books have been approved by our therapists. If you want to read something else, you can ask for it, but you need to run it by your therapist first.'

I've already had my magazines taken off me. They are 'unhelpful' to ladies in recovery. This place is serious.

I hunker down in a corner and shield my eyes with my hand. I don't want to catch anyone's sideways glances. The girls talk to each other a little, but I don't really hear their words. I'm trapped in this surreal place and I don't want to be here but I don't want to go home . . . I don't want to be anywhere.

A bell rings, and Nicola, a mental health technician (MHT) who has been assigned to look after me since I'm on 'eyesight' (one-to-one observation), leads me to another low building where there is a dining area. It's bright and airy and decorated with various pieces of artwork, but I hardly notice. I sit at a table with about six other girls. We are called one by one to a counter where we are given our meals by a squeaky-voiced redhead who believes in service with a smile.

Once we have all been served, Abbie stands up to say grace. I keep my eyes open in defiance.

Then Nicola asks if anyone has anything they want to talk about over dinner. The table is silent. She turns to me.

'Sharon, some ladies struggle with mealtimes here at New Beginnings, so we like to support each other. Sometimes we don't feel like conversation and it's easier if we play a game. Do you want to do the Alphabet Game, girls?'

There are a few nods around the table.

'Right, I'll start, and we'll go clockwise. Here's a topic – female singers! Okay, A is for Agnetha from ABBA. That's double points! Sue, you're next.'

'B is for Beyoncé.'

'C is for Cher.'

It's my turn.

'I don't want to play.'

'That's okay, Sharon, since you've just arrived, but we hope you will join in, in time.'

'D is for Dionne Warwick.'

The game continues until they get to J. Then a moment of awkwardness ensues.

'K is for Karen Carpenter.'

Half of the girls at the table have anorexia. There are a couple of giggles. Nicola clears her throat.

'Ahem. Moving swiftly on.'

I find myself settling into the rhythm of the game and the meal. Some of the girls dissect their food slowly, but eventually we have all finished.

'You can have a cup of coffee since you haven't left anything on your plate. Take your tray back to Lisa.'

Lisa is the squeaky redhead. She gives me a large mug of coffee and offers a selection of flavoured creamers. This is new to me, but there's no milk. I choose hazelnut. But there's something wrong with the coffee. I need a buzz that's not forthcoming.

Sue notices my expression.

'It's decaf. We only get real coffee in the morning.'

That explains it. I am going to have an enforced caffeine detox too.

When all the tables have handed in their trays, it seems that one small girl, Lori – the frightened one with the big eyes – hasn't been able to finish. Lisa brings out an Ensure high-calorie drink and Abbie measures some out carefully into a glass. She's looking at some kind of table and working out how much equates to what Lori has left.

Lori hesitates. The other girls encourage her. 'You can do it.' 'It's worth it for your recovery.'

But she's still struggling, so Abbie pours another glass and takes hold of it herself.

'Let's do this together!'

To cheers and clapping, both of them down the Ensure at the same time. My jaw drops open. I've never seen a nurse do that before.

Then another MHT, Corey, raps her table.

'Now we all know it's somebody's birthday.'

A girl sitting beside her with green eyes and dark curls blushes bright red and everyone looks round at her.

'Time for birthday affirmations! Sue, will you take the pen.'

Sue stands up by a flip chart opened at a new page, marker poised to write.

Someone shouts out, 'Mia is a good friend.'

'Mia is someone you can talk to when you're down.'

'Mia is beautiful like a butterfly!'

'I like it when Mia smiles.'

This is weird. Very weird. I feel a little warmth in my belly, but it doesn't last. Mia is my roommate, but I am not sharing with her at the moment. Ladies on 'eyesight' sleep on a sofa bed in the common room.

We stay in the dining room for a while after dinner. There are couches in one corner, and a few of the girls sit there and get out some cards.

'Do you want to play Nertz, Sharon?'

'I don't know how.'

'We'll teach you.'

'No thanks.'

Jenny, a chubbier girl with dimpled cheeks, sits down at an electric piano I hadn't noticed by the door. She starts to play an old hymn. I recognize it as 'Jesus Paid it All'. It irks me somehow. What have these girls got to do with God? I can see how unwell some of them are. It's written all over their faces. Abusive families, abusive relationships, pressure to perform, financial crises . . . or simply the impact of severe mental illness. I can't see where God is in all of this. How can they?

* * *

The golf cart stops at the top of the hill, opposite the chapel. The other girls hop off and walk up the steps to its doors.

'Sharon?'

Corey has been driving. She looks at me with raised eyebrows.

'I'm not going.'

'You have to, honey. All the girls do. It's part of the programme.'

The programme. Everything bows to the programme.

I look towards the grazing horses in the paddock by the driveway. I'd rather spend time with them than with a God who has neglected me. The scene is so much more peaceful than the landscape of my thoughts.

'Come on. I'll walk in with you.'

I drag my heels as I cross the road. I can hear music coming from the sanctuary. I stumble in and sit on a hard bench at the very back against the wall.

The worship leader is a curly haired girl in her late twenties. Her voice is pure and carries above the congregated staff and patients. She's singing a worship song I recognize, though probably from the radio – I've never sung it before. It's about God's mercy and how he fights for our hearts.

Many of the women are singing; some with hands raised, open; some are swaying; some dancing inappropriately energetically. Oh yes, an opportunity to burn calories with impunity.

But, for most, the worship seems real. These women, struggling with eating disorders, depression, self-harm – women with a history of abuse, broken relationships, suicide attempts and trauma – are singing to God with conviction that nothing can separate them from him. Nothing? Do they really believe it?

It's so long since I've been in a church and it is overwhelming. I feel a sudden surge of emotion. I start to cry and it's not just a silent tear rolling down my cheek. Here I am, my heart so restless, so ill at ease. I have been so defiant, so resentful of my illness. Could it be that God actually loves me enough to fight for my hardened heart? Could it be true that nothing – not even my bitter profession of hatred for him – can prevail over God's faithfulness to me?

I try to contain myself, but the great, heaving sobs keep coming. I glance up and catch Corey looking at me. There are tears in her eyes too. She moves to sit beside me, puts a gentle hand on my shoulder, offers me a packet of tissues. I accept them gratefully.

The worship leader sings the refrain again and again with passion and purpose. It speaks of God's grace and how he extends it to each one of us. Grace. For me? I feel my heart beat faster and faster.

The singing continues for a while and then there is a short sermon, but I don't hear it. I am too absorbed in this thought: God wants me back. He has been wrestling me to the point of surrender. Like Jacob in the book of Genesis, I have encountered God and I am weakened, 'limping'. Yet Jacob left with a blessing, and I feel as though I too have been blessed. My racing heart has softened.

The service ends and the girls start to file out, but I don't move. Some of them glance at me as they pass by. My sobs have slowed but I am still a wretched sight, hair wet, eyes red from crying.

'Are you okay?'

Corey's voice is soft. I nod and try to smile, but my facial muscles are too tight.

'Come on, let's catch this golf cart.'

7

Sighing out my bitterness
Wrestling with despair

It's midnight. I am still on 'eyesight', so a nurse, Leah, sits at my bedside. The light is low but I can see enough to make out some of the Native American artwork on the walls and the wooden plaques engraved with Scripture verses. There really is no escaping the gospel in this place.

I sit up for a second, almost wrenching from my nose the tube that delivers my night-time feed.

Leah looks up from the book she has borrowed from the library in the corner.

'You can't sleep, honey?'

I haven't slept since I arrived, even with the tranquillizers I am taking. I shake my head.

'Would you like a book to read?'

'No, thanks.'

I look at my hands. They are trembling. So is my lip. I can't get what happened in the chapel out of my mind. I have felt God's presence for the first time in months and I desperately want to hold on to it. I recall the days when I was so passionate about my faith, when it was so central to everything that I did. They seem so distant. I have denied Christ and blamed God for so much.

'Leah?'

'Yes, honey?'

'Are you a Christian?'

I know that she is. There's something about her – about most of the staff here – that speaks of peace and faith and hope and love.

'Yes, I am. Why do you ask?'

'I don't know. I mean . . .'

Leah closes her book and looks at me earnestly.

'. . . I've been thinking about stuff – about faith, I guess. It's hard not to here, you know? I've drifted so far from God, but something happened in chapel today that made me wonder . . .'

'Wonder what, sweetheart?'

'You know – whether he would take me back.'

Leah smiles.

'Sharon, he doesn't need to take you back. You once gave your life to him, didn't you?'

'Yes.'

'Do you remember the Bible passage where Jesus tells the people that he is the Good Shepherd?'

'Ye-es.'

She reaches for the Bible on the bedside table.

'It's in John 10. Here, look. This is Jesus speaking: "My sheep listen to my voice; I know them, and they follow me. I give them eternal life, and they shall never perish; no one will snatch them out of my hand."'[1]

Nothing will snatch them. That song is still playing in my head: nothing – absolutely nothing – can stand between God and me.

My mind is working overtime. So is my heart.

'You are one of those sheep, sweetie. Jesus is your Saviour, your Shepherd. And he loves you.'

'But – but I've felt so far from him.'

I drop my voice.

'I said I hated him.'

'Sharon, do you remember what happened to the apostle Peter at the time of Jesus' arrest before he was crucified? Peter denied Jesus three times. He claimed he had nothing to do with him. He swore that he did not know Jesus. But what did Jesus do? He forgave him everything and told him to feed his lambs.'

Tears are spilling onto my cheeks.

'He will forgive you too, honey. And I believe he has a job for you to do – just like Peter would take care of his sheep.'

I am staring at a plaque on the wall opposite my bed. It has Jeremiah 29:11 engraved on it: '"For I know the plans I have for you," declares the LORD, "plans to prosper you and not to harm you, plans to give you hope and a future."'

Leah follows my gaze.

'That promise is for you, you know.'

Yes, although, remembering the context, the Israelites the Lord was addressing in Jeremiah went through a lot of troubled times before they even caught a glimpse of that better future, didn't they? I play with the tasselled trim of my blanket.

'Do you remember the parable of the prodigal son in the Gospels?'

I nod.

'What happens at the end? The father doesn't just wait for his wayward son to come home; he runs to him with arms open wide. I believe he's running towards you right now, hun. All you have to do is allow his love to enfold you.'

There is silence for a moment as I process all my thoughts and emotions. This is for real. I know that God wants me back, and I want him too.

'Leah, will you pray with me?'

'Sure. What do you want to pray?'

'Just that God would accept me. I want to give my life back to him.'

Leah beams and squeezes my hand.

'Of course. How about I get Irma to join us? I'm sure she would love to pray with you too.'

I can just see Irma through the open door. She's at the nurses' station in the hallway, writing some notes.

Leah calls her in and she draws another chair towards my bed.

Soon we are praying together and I am crying, but it's different now. I feel lighter, freer, as I recommit my life to God in the presence of these two witnesses. I breathe in God's love and sigh out all my bitterness.

We cry together; we laugh together.

Irma gets called away to tend to another patient, but Leah keeps my left hand in her right as she urges me to try to get some sleep.

The hands of the clock turn and still I am awake, but I am at peace. I know that I am still very ill. I know that I have a lot of work to do in therapy. But I also know that I am no longer fighting my depression on my own. God has wrestled with my heart and filled me anew with the truth of his grace. I am in the palm of his hand and my illness is not going to snatch me from it.

It seems like a turning point. Could I be on the road to recovery?

* * *

Everything has changed, and nothing has changed.

After breakfast, I participate in the morning prayer time.

'Lord, please help all those who are struggling today. Let them know your presence with them. Thank you that you care for each one of us . . .'

I open my eyes for a split second and catch Nicola and Abbie exchanging glances. When we are all finished, about six sets of eyes are trained on me. Jenny's mouth is hanging open.

Throughout the day, I wear a smile, and it seems like every member of staff is eager to return it, sharing in my joy. I have a new glow inside. But by late afternoon I can feel the familiar heavy cloud descend on my shoulders once more. The lower half of my face is still smiling, but my eyes deaden and I can feel the concertina of my wrinkled brow.

Was it real? Or was it all hyped-up emotion?

I have shown for twenty-four hours that I can be responsible for my own safety, so my psychiatrist, Dr Bernstein, lifts the 'eyesight' order, which means that I can sleep in my bedroom again.

Mia is thankful for my company. She is not a good sleeper either. We chat in the small hours of the morning, exchanging stories of how we came to be at the ranch, and finding that we have so much in common that we both know we will be friends for life.

In the end, my eyes grow heavy and I descend into a murky dreamworld filled with shadowy figures and distorted faces. When

Irma rouses me, I am disorientated. I realize that I am clenching my fists and my jaw.

'Good morning, Sharon. Hi, Mia.'

Mia has already showered and is in her gown, ready to be weighed. We are all weighed every morning, but only the nurses can see the display; we are to be 'blind' to our numbers until the treatment team feels that we are ready to accept our new bodies.

The blankets feel heavy on my legs. My left arm is damp and sticky: my nasogastric tube has detached from the bag of yellow nutrient-rich fluid hanging beside me. It is still dripping.

I groan.

Mia sees what has happened and calls Irma, who rushes back.

'What a mess, huh, honey! Let's get you cleaned up.'

She locks the bag of feed and detaches the tube completely.

'You go and shower off, hun, and I'll change your bed for you.'

'Thanks.'

I blunder towards the shower, clumsy from insomnia and still half submerged in a dark dreamscape.

We have some quiet time before breakfast and I lift *The Message* from the library shelf. If I'm going to be a proper Christian, I had better live like it. I turn to a passage in Matthew 11 that resonated with me in my student days.

Are you tired? Worn out? Burned out on religion? Come to me. Get away with me and you'll recover your life. I'll show you how to take a real rest. Walk with me and work with me – watch how I do it. Learn the unforced rhythms of grace. I won't lay anything heavy or ill-fitting on you. Keep company with me and you'll learn to live freely and lightly.
(Matthew 11:28–30, *The Message*)

Rest. Unforced rhythms. Freely and lightly. I sigh and put the book back on the shelf.

'Are you okay?'

Nicola pushes her fringe out of her eyes.

I shrug. I'm thinking through soup again.

The bell rings and we file out, crossing the yard to the dining room. Mia sits beside me. She twists her hair with her left hand and twirls her spoon with her right.

'Mia, what would help you right now? Shall we all play a game?'

Nicola is upbeat. No one seems to share her enthusiasm.

'I know how you're feeling, Mia.'

It's Lori.

'Remember how I struggled the other day? I know it's so hard, but you can do it.'

Mia grimaces but spoons some fruit loops into her mouth, chewing awkwardly.

I eat my banana and peanut butter tortilla mindlessly. I stare through the window, seeing nothing.

I finish, earning my coffee. It tastes really good with hazelnut creamer, and jolts me back to the room. I smile at Mia, who is finishing her toast with a resigned expression.

It's prayer time again. Nicola begins.

'Thank you, Lord, for this bright new morning. Thank you that your mercies are new every day, that this really is a place of New Beginnings. Thank you that these women are here and that they can have the hope of healing. Thank you for Lori, for Mia, for Jenny, for Sharon . . .'

She works round the room, making sure that she misses no one. A silence follows.

'Ahem.'

Jenny clears her throat.

'Jesus, thank you for Sharon being able to come here all the way from Ireland, and thank you for what you are doing in her life.'

Her prayer is short, but I shift uncomfortably. This morning it seems as though God is not close. But faith is not about feelings, I remind myself. Still, I don't feel like praying this time. Neither does anyone else, so Abbie closes up.

'Amen and amen.'

I walk back to our house. There's fifteen minutes before our first group, so I take a chair outside to sit for a moment. We have to be indoors between ten and four, so I want to make the most of the Arizona sun.

'Sharon. SShharon!'

One of the older patients, Luisa, is seated on a bench close by.

'Sharon, don't move!'

I look around me.

'Under your seat! It's under your seat – a rattler!'

I stiffen. My eyes plead with Luisa for help.

'Stay there. I'll get someone!'

But I can't. Slowly, I stand up, then walk steadily towards the door of the house. I swing it shut behind me and slide down the wall to the floor, heart pounding.

Luisa follows me in. Her cheeks are flushed.

'You are so lucky! If that thing had bitten . . .'

I know. Maybe I am meant to be alive after all.

* * *

I meet with my primary therapist in the shade of a gazebo. Both of us like the outdoors, and there is a breeze today – warm but pleasant. We are in the middle of a garden of cacti and succulents, and a hummingbird hovers close by.

Rick and I sit in silence for what seems like several minutes. He observes my demeanour with gentle eyes.

'The darkness is back.'

I nod.

'It's still real, you know – what happened.'

I look towards the forest of tall saguaro cacti on the hillside to my right.

Rick sets down his files and his Bible. He tells me that I am a daughter of the King, and that nothing can change that.

I shift my weight on my wicker chair. My face is set halfway between a smile and a frown.

'Tell me what's going on for you.'

'I don't know. I mean, I don't feel like I can do this.'

'Do what?'

'Life. My life. The other girls have hope. They're different. I have this – this presence with me. It never leaves.'

'You're right, you know. In a sense. You're dealing with more than some of the others. Even from what we've talked about so far – there are complexities . . .'

'I wish God would just send his angels to take me home.'

Rick swallows and clasps his hands together.

'That makes me feel sad, Sharon. Because, you know, I see a great future for you. You're perceptive, you think about things, you have depth and more strength than you know.'

I shake my head.

'Tell me, what would you want for your life if you didn't have this depression? Where would you see yourself?'

'I can't see myself without depression.'

'Cos I've been thinking about this psalm – this verse I want to share with you. It's Psalm 37 verse 4.'

There's a bookmark in his Bible. He opens it, but barely needs to look down.

'"Take delight in the LORD, and he will give you the desires of your heart." Sharon, that promise is for you. God wants to give you your heart's desires as you delight yourself in him.'

I breathe in and out slowly and audibly.

'I don't know what my heart desires. I don't think it desires anything.'

'But what would it desire if you weren't depressed?'

'I don't even want to not be depressed any more. This is just me. It's who I am.'

Rick uncrosses his ankles and sits up straight.

'You know, I've never heard anyone say that before.'

'Say what?'

'That they actually want to hang on to their depression. It makes me sad that that is your identity.'

I feel pressure at the back of my eyes. I guess it is sad, but I am too numb to actually cry.

'I still think this verse is for you. I think you need to delight your-self in the Lord first, and then he will reveal your heart's desires.'

'I guess.'

My stomach tightens. I feel as if I exist on two planes. On the one hand, I have become aware again of God's presence; on the other, I am still almost consumed by darkness. There is a downward force tugging at me. My thin frame feels heavy.

'You're tired. Let's walk back together.'

I lift my little black folder and stand up in assent.

'It's beautiful here, isn't it?'

'Yes.'

'There's something about the desert. It's raw and wild and open.'

I nod. I see the beauty, but I feel disconnected from it.

We reach the door of Navajo House.

'I'll be praying for you, Sharon, if that's okay.'

I lift my head.

'Thanks.'

* * *

The days go by. I follow the programme. I go to individual therapy, I go to group therapy, I go to nutrition classes and psychology appointments and reviews with my psychiatrist. I comply with medication changes, even after a serious drug reaction that necessitates a stay in the nearby general hospital. I get to know – and really care about – the other women on the programme. I appreciate the skill and wisdom of the dietitians and nurses and MHTs.

I talk a lot about my problems, but I don't feel like I am finding solutions. I gain weight and become physically healthier, but mentally I am stuck.

I try to engage, try to contribute and speak helpfully into the lives of others and pray and read and learn. At one stage someone calls me a 'New Beginnings miracle'.

But my therapists know that darkness simmers beneath the surface. And, in time, it boils over.

We're in an early-morning group therapy session – six of us, with two therapists facilitating. As usual, we start with a 'feelings check-in', with each person sharing their main emotions so that everyone knows where everyone else is at.

The therapists begin.

'I feel hopeful this morning.'

'Funny, that's what I was going to say too. It must be in the air today. Lori, your turn.'

'I feel disappointed.'

'Okay, we can talk about that in a minute. Mia, what about you?'

'I feel scared.'

'Yes, you felt a bit like that yesterday too, didn't you? Sharon?'

'I feel suicidal.'

The room is silent. Rick and Dana exchange glances. Rick speaks.

'Sharon, "suicidal" is not an emotion. There has to be a feeling – or feelings – underlying that thought. Can you think of any?'

'No. I can't.'

'Jenny, would you please pass the feelings card to Sharon?'

She hands over a laminated list of 'feeling words', from 'happy' and 'joyful' to 'disillusioned' and 'afraid'. I look at them, but nothing resonates. I set it down and shrug.

'Are you sad? Perhaps angry?'

I shake my head. My whole body stiffens.

'You look like you might be feeling angry . . .'

'I just want to die.'

Rick sits forward in the sofa.

'Sharon, just come outside with me for a second.'

I follow him through the door. We stand in the shade.

Rick's voice is low.

'Sharon, I know . . . I know you're despairing. But you've agreed to the group guidelines. We must always be mindful of others in the group before we share something, right?'

I nod.

'Well, Lori is crying in there. What you're saying is upsetting. We are open and honest, but there is a place for holding back. You know you can talk about anything in your individual sessions, but I need you to be careful in the group, okay?'

He's kind.

I nod again.

'I'm sorry.'

'That's okay. I think it's better if I take you back over to Abbie. I'm going to suggest that we keep you on "eyesight" for a day or two – until you feel less desperate.'

I shuffle my feet and choke back tears.

I'm no miracle. I'm the greatest failure who ever lived.

8
Too alive
Wrestling with suicidal thoughts

It's raining. No more blue skies or towering cacti. I'm back at home and I've learnt so much from New Beginnings, so why am I not feeling better?

Perhaps now that my real problems are not masked by dangerous skinniness, I'm in a good place to get help. But I'm not hopeful. Everyone is pleased that I am maintaining a healthy body weight. What they don't realize is that the numbness that comes from starvation has gone. The pain of my depression has never been so acute.

I still believe that I have encountered God. I'm convinced of this, and I do long to be closer to him, but it feels as if the darkness that surrounds me is difficult even for the Holy Spirit to penetrate. I find it hard to go to church, but a loyal friend takes me to a 'Freedom in Christ' course in a café. I try desperately to internalize the truths it teaches – in Christ, I am far from oppression and will not live in fear (see Isaiah 54:14); in Christ, I overcome the enemy of my soul by the blood of the Lamb and the word of my testimony (see Revelation 12:11) – but somehow the darkness seems to prevail. I feel oppressed; I feel as though the 'enemy of my soul' is present and active.

A woman from the church running the course starts to pray with me. She prays for deliverance from evil, for the demolition of strongholds. Each week I return and am no better. She asks me if

I am harbouring unconfessed sins in my heart. I don't think I am. Am I really allowing the devil to control me, to establish strongholds that need to be broken? Is that why I am still so ill? I don't think so, but I start to have doubts about the reality of my salvation. I decide that the prayer ministry is doing me more harm than good. I thank the lady graciously and stop going.

Other girls leaving New Beginnings are doing so with entire after-care teams in place – a psychiatrist, a dietitian, a therapist, perhaps a psychologist and a recovery coach. I have come home with nothing. I am on the waiting list to see a psychiatrist, but I have no idea when I will get an assessment. In the meantime, my GP, Dr Oates, quickly recognizes my predicament and starts to fit in weekly (sometimes even twice-weekly) appointments so that I have some kind of consistent support. She is excellent, and I build my whole life around those ten- or twenty-minute visits to the surgery.

The senior (semi-retired) pastor from my own church starts to take me out for a coffee and a chat every week. I feel reassured in his godly presence. When he realizes that it is helping me, he organizes a rota so that there is someone from church for me to meet with every weekday. It feels a little contrived at times – the people I have coffee with are not really my 'friends' – but I appreciate the support, and the prospect of company at 2 pm often gets me through a hard morning. I start to feel the love of God, but I am still desperately low.

* * *

I lie on my back on my sofa, tears running down my cheeks. It is mid-afternoon in May, but my apartment is dark. I have closed all the heavy curtains, closed myself off from the world.

A letter lies open on the table beside me. It is printed on the General Medical Council's headed paper. I have applied for a licence to practise medicine. After all, I am a qualified doctor. Could realizing that dream lift me from the depths – give me a purpose and a new identity?

Apparently not. The GMC assessors have read my submission, considered my psychiatric history and all the medication that I take, and have concluded:

> In the present circumstances, we consider that, as a doctor, you would pose a potential danger to patients. We are also concerned about the risk that practising medicine would expose you to personally . . . We consider you unfit to practise; however, should your health stabilise for a period of two years, we would be willing to consider your case afresh.

A potential danger to patients. A potential danger to patients. The words turn over and over in my head. It hurts. I went to medical school because I cared about patients – I was passionate about helping people in vulnerable situations. I don't care about the risk to me personally. My life doesn't matter. But to be seen as a risk to others? It cuts me to the core.

I wipe my face with a damp tissue and pull my knees up to my chest. There is ringing in my ears and my back aches. I am unfit to practise medicine. I am unfit for anything else.

I feel a sudden surge of energy. I don't have to suffer this pain. There's always a way out . . .

No. No, don't think like that . . .

But –

It's too final . . .

I want it to be final.

God doesn't want that for you . . .

God surely doesn't want me to feel this pain.

The internal argument rages for an hour. Eventually, I pick up my phone and tap in the number of a suicide helpline my GP has recommended, but I hang up when someone answers. I don't really want to be talked out of it.

* * *

It's midnight, and I am sitting up, very much alive – much too alive, in fact – on a trolley in the Accident and Emergency Department. Six or seven kidney dishes filled with bile surround me. My head is spinning and sore, and I'm still retching.

I hear a child screaming in the next cubicle, an alarm beeping down the corridor. Nurses rush to and fro. I can just see their feet as they pass.

A doctor pulls back the curtain, notes in hand. She was in my year group at uni, but she doesn't acknowledge it. She barely acknowledges me at all, surveying the mess instead.

'Are you feeling sick?'

Obviously.

'Yes, very.'

She doesn't offer to give me anything for it.

'Your blood results are not good. You'll be going upstairs. And I need to put this in your arm.'

She takes a fine-bore cannula from a tray and a tourniquet from her pocket. She washes her hands in the sink at the corner and then looks for a good vein. I'm dehydrated and there aren't any, but somehow she manages to get it in at my elbow crease anyway.

I expect the usual questions – 'Did you intend to die? Do you regret what you did?' – but they don't follow. Maybe they are going to send a psychiatrist to assess me instead.

The doctor runs her hand through her hair and purses her lips, scribbling something on the notes and reversing out of the cubicle.

No psychiatrist arrives, but a motherly nursing assistant comes in and clears up the kidney dishes. She looks me in the eye as if to say 'You shouldn't have done this', but then gives my arm a gentle squeeze. I feel tears welling up for the first time. What is it that I have done? I thought I had taken enough . . . But the blood results? Maybe I have and it's going to be a long and agonizing death.

Some time passes. I can hear a commotion from the resuscitation area. Someone has suffered a cardiac arrest, perhaps, or maybe they've received the victims of a traffic accident. I won't get much attention for a while. I don't feel worthy of anyone's attention. I caused this. I messed up.

A nurse comes in, wheeling a drip stand in one hand and carrying a medicine cup in the other.

'You're to get fluids and I need you to take these.'

She hands me the pills. An antidote.

For a moment I consider refusing them, but I realize that my blood tests have probably shown organ damage. If I am going to live, I should probably allow them to treat that. The nurse gives me a drink of water and I swallow. She attaches a bag of fluids to my cannula and starts the drip.

'There's a bed for you in Ward Four. I've bleeped the porters, so they should be here soon to take you up.'

'Thanks.'

What else do I say? I don't want to go to Ward Four. I don't want to go anywhere. And I definitely don't want anyone to know what has happened.

The porter, who clearly has no idea of the reason for my admission, is bright and breezy.

'Right, love, can you hop over into the chair for me? We'll get you upstairs and feeling better in no time.'

As we ascend in the lift, he whistles a tune I recognize but can't place.

'Here we are. This is the medical ward. Ah, Trudy, I've got your patient for you.'

Trudy looks me up and down. Her smile is unconvincing.

'Thanks, Bert. She's in bed five.'

Bert helps me out of the chair and hands my bag of fluids to Trudy, who attaches it to a drip stand that is waiting by the bed.

'All the best, love.'

Trudy pulls the curtain around me. Most of the patients are sleeping, but there's one lady by the window who has an awful hacking cough and is sitting upright, trying to get a breath.

'I just have to fill out some admission papers with you, but we'll get through them quickly so you can get some sleep.'

She asks me who my next of kin is and whether I want them to be notified. I don't. Most of the rest of the pack is irrelevant. I don't have mobility and care needs, and I can make my own way to the toilet. Do I want to see a chaplain? Not in these circumstances. For the first time, I feel real shame.

Trudy leaves me, but I can overhear her conversation with two nursing assistants at their station just outside the six-bed bay.

'Yes, that's the overdose in now.'

'Isn't it just awful? Mr Farquhar had to go to that outlying bed because some wee flossie's been running all over Belfast, taking this, taking that . . .'

Some wee flossie. Not just unfit to practise. Not just a failed doctor. But 'some wee flossie'.

My cheeks burn and my leg muscles twitch. How the mighty have fallen.

Suicide in severe mental illness: the statistics

- During an episode of depression in major depressive disorder, the risk that someone will attempt suicide is twenty-one times that of the general population.[1]
- Suicide rates are eight to ten times higher in people with bipolar disorder compared with the general population.[2]
- 10% of patients with schizophrenia commit suicide (with as many as 50% attempting it at least once).[3]

9

Aftercare. At last
Wrestling with my body

Several sleepless hours later, and the medical doctor arrives with an entourage of four. He is tall, and his face is square. One of his trainees pulls the curtains round. I sit up in the bed.

'Good morning.'

'Good morning.'

'My name is Dr Black. I gather you are a colleague.'

My tongue is stuck to the roof of my mouth. I nod, half-heartedly.

'Then you will understand what I mean when I tell you your liver enzymes are very high. We will have to watch to make sure they fall again over the next few days.'

'Mm-hmm.'

My brain feels gritty and I can smell chemicals inside my upper airways.

'You are very lucky that you were so sick. It may have saved you, you know. We had a sixteen-year-old last week who wasn't so fortunate.'

There's a lump in my throat. I wipe a tear from my left eye.

'Who is your psychiatrist?'

'I don't have one – I'm, uh, on the waiting list.'

'Well, I'd like you to see one before you leave here. There is a consultant here, a Dr Harris, who I think might be able to help you.'

He turns to the junior who is waiting, pen poised, to make notes.

'Dr Graham, could you make that referral please?'

Dr Graham assents and scribbles something.

'I'm very sorry that you felt so desperate. Do you feel that you can stay safe on this ward?'

The thought that this Dr Harris might be able to help me has somehow given me hope. I feel more ashamed than despairing.

'Yes.'

'Then let's keep those fluids running. You can eat when you feel like it. We'll repeat the bloods daily and see which way this goes.'

He starts to push the curtain back.

'I will see you tomorrow morning.'

'Thank you.'

I spend three long days in the medical ward, thinking about what I have done, veering between wishing it had worked and hoping that – with the right help coming along – I might actually be able to live a meaningful life again.

My liver enzymes fall, and I am medically fit for discharge. I am given an appointment with Dr Harris for the following Monday.

A friend from my church rings me and I tell her what has happened. I am relieved that she does not condemn me. Instead, she offers me a lift home and says that if I want to go to the service on Sunday, she will go with me. I'm not ready for that, but I thank her anyway.

* * *

It's Monday. I don't feel like driving to my appointment with Dr Harris, so I take the bus and walk from the city centre to the complex of temporary buildings beside the hospital, where I have been told she has her office.

My knees wobble as I walk. I recall that first psychiatry appointment three years ago when I had no idea what to expect. This feels similar.

Dr Harris is running nearly an hour late, and I am about to give up when she pops her head around the waiting room door.

'Sharon?'

I lift my bag from the floor and follow her. She is red-haired, squat, and walks with a slight limp.

We sit opposite each other in a small office with piles of notes lining one wall.

'Well, Dr Black has spoken to me about you, so you don't need to go over the details of what happened last week. I just want to hear what has been going on for you generally and how you are feeling today.'

I take a deep breath and begin to tell the story of my depression, doing finals while in hospital, going to England, going to America, and coming home feeling so lost and alone. I end by telling her how I tried to redeem the situation by getting licensed as a doctor, and about the GMC letter that dashed all my hopes in that regard.

Dr Harris does a lot of nodding and frowning and says 'Aha' several times. At the end of the story, she looks me squarely in the eye.

'I think I can help you, Sharon – if you're willing to work with me. Are you willing to work with me?'

I've barely met her but there's something about her determined manner that encourages me.

'Yes. I'm willing.'

'Well, I'm a psychotherapist as well as a psychiatrist. I can offer you talking therapy, but I will review your drugs as well. I gather no one has done that since you left the States. Can you make it here for eight-thirty in the morning? I can see you again on Friday.'

'Yes.'

It's all happening rather quickly after such a long wait. I'm almost glad I ended up in hospital.

'We'll meet at least once a week, and you will assure me of your safety in between times.'

I nod. Aftercare. At last.

What is a psychotherapist?
A psychotherapist uses 'psychoanalytic' or 'psychodynamic' techniques in the context of a long-term therapeutic relationship.

According to the British Psychoanalytic Council, psychotherapy is:

A therapeutic process which helps patients understand and resolve their problems by increasing awareness of their inner world and its influence over relationships both past and present. It differs from most other therapies in aiming for deep-seated change in personality and emotional development.[1]

Simply put, the patient speaks in free association, allowing subconscious thoughts to surface. The psychotherapist remarks on these, helping the patient to make connections and begin to understand his or her own personality. There is some evidence for the effectiveness of this type of psychotherapy as an adjunctive intervention in treating psychosis, but the studies involved have limitations.[2]

After a few weeks of seeing Dr Harris as an outpatient, she decides to admit me to the ward. My depression is unrelenting, and she wants to change my medication.

It's a different unit from the one I was in previously, and I realize from the outset that I am going to like it a lot better. I have my own room, the nurses are very attentive and the occupational therapists are energetic, making sure that I don't have too much time to overthink.

Dr Harris is not an inpatient consultant, but I go to her office twice a week and she sends me back with a note for Dr McKay in the ward, suggesting this change or that. My antidepressant is changed and one of the drugs for anxiety is stopped.

I start to feel better surprisingly quickly. Much better. So much better, in fact, that when the occupational therapists take me shopping, I buy two party dresses – one green, one black and white with great big polka dots – and start to wear them in the ward along with bright green eyeshadow and pink lipstick.

One morning, I go to see Dr Harris wearing the green dress with a pair of heels. She raises her eyebrows.

'How are you feeling, Sharon?'

'I feel great. Super. Wonderful, in fact. This medication is so much better.'

'And those thoughts that life is not worth living – where are you at with those now?'

'They're gone. I don't think I'll ever think that again. I think I can go home now. Don't you?'

'Hmmm. I think we'll just keep an eye on things for a bit, shall we?'

I can see what she is writing on the notes in front of her.

'Sharon's demeanour is quite altered. I am concerned that she is becoming hypomanic . . .'

She pauses for a second, then strikes out the word 'hypomanic' and writes 'elated' instead. She is not ready to make a new diagnosis. Yet.

As it happens, my hypomania/elation seems to settle over the next week or two. I tone down the eyeshadow and revert to wearing jeans and a T-shirt, but the depression has definitely lifted. I have more and more leave from the ward on my own, and, in time, Dr McKay discharges me.

I continue seeing Dr Harris as an outpatient. She is eccentric, but I like her. We talk about all sorts of things – many seemingly irrelevant – and it helps. With her support, I start a part-time work placement as a receptionist in a mattress factory, and I start to feel a sense of purpose in life again.

But one day, something strange happens to me. I am walking to see Dr Harris and it's a freezing cold October morning, but I'm sweating profusely and I arrive in soaking wet clothes.

She thinks I might have flu and sends me home to bed, but I don't have any symptoms except that I seem to shiver when the heat is on in my apartment and break out in a sweat when it is cold. That night, I have to change my pyjamas seven times, and I end up changing the bedclothes as well.

This goes on for several days, and I start to leave a pile of eight or nine folded camisoles by my bed, ready for all the changes that I will go through in the course of the night.

My GP does blood tests which eliminate some of the scariest causes of night sweats, but sends me to an infectious diseases consultant just in case I caught something unusual in Arizona.

At the hospital, the doctor identifies a five-centimetre inflammatory mass under my chin which I've never noticed before. She aspirates fluid from its centre with a fine needle and finds pus cells, so she admits me to the ward for intravenous antibiotics. Once the infection has been treated, she makes arrangements for a head and neck surgeon to remove the mass.

In the interim, no one can tell me whether this lump is benign or malignant. I realize that just a couple of months ago, I wouldn't have cared. Why is it that now, when I want to live, when I'm not depressed, this should happen to me? I cry into my pillow. It doesn't seem fair.

I miss seeing Dr Harris for several weeks. I'm weak, and the sweats make it difficult to go anywhere. But mentally, I am okay. In spite of what I am going through, that sense of despair is gone.

I have the surgery and it turns out that the tumour is benign. The sweats don't stop automatically, and for the first time my infectious diseases consultant suggests that they might have nothing to do with this lump. She has been reading about the drugs I am taking and those that were stopped in the summer, and she thinks I might be going through withdrawal.

Whatever the cause, the sweats ease in time and I start to get into a simple routine at home. I walk to the corner shop in the morning to get a newspaper, go home and read it – often cover to cover – spend some time connecting online with my friends from New Beginnings, or have a coffee with one of my church friends in a little café very close to my apartment, rest in the afternoon and watch TV in the evening. I eat regularly, sleep for eight hours, sweats notwithstanding, and start to see Dr Harris again.

And it dawns on me one day that this is what it actually feels like to be well. I am ready to make a fresh start in life, perhaps look at reception work again.

But can it last?

10

More than well
Wrestling with mania

'Snow, snow! I lo-o-ve snow! "Good King Wenceslas looked out on the Feast of Stephen . . ."'[1]

I am singing at the top of my lungs. Less than tunefully.

'Ha! Just a little bit taller, a little bit fatter here . . .'

An elderly lady who lives in the apartment next to mine pops her head around the exterior door.

'Sharon, are you – uh – okay?'

'Oh, Mrs Spencer, I'm more than okay! I feel spectacular! Isn't the garden beautiful today?'

'But what are you doing?'

'Can't you see? I know he has no head yet, but I'm building a snowman. My biggest snowman ever! He's going to be seven feet tall. I'm calling him Trevor!'

'Mmm-eh-hmm. It's very cold. Don't you want a hat?'

'I'm warmer than I've ever been in my entire life, thanks, Mrs Spencer.'

I'm rolling a big ball of snow as I speak. I stop, breathless, and laugh out loud.

'Okay, then.'

She is about to retreat. I stop her.

'Do you have a carrot? I've got buttons for his eyes but I want him to have a proper snowman's nose. A nose he can be proud of!'

'I think so . . .'

She raises her eyebrows and exhales through pursed lips, then retreats.

I resume my song and roll Trevor's head a little more. I am just setting it on to the enormous body when Mrs Spencer returns.

'Sorry, I've only got a parsnip. Here.'

'A parsnip is perfect. Perfect parsnips, a parsnip is perfectamundo!'

'I've brought you a scarf too.'

'Ooooh! Trevor will look so suave in that.'

'Eh? It wasn't for the snowman. You'll catch pneumonia with that open jacket.'

Mrs Spencer sighs and leaves me to it. I pat plenty more snow around Trevor's neck. I don't want his head to fall off. There! I'm satisfied. I wrap the rather expensive-looking scarf around him and make a knot at the front.

'"When the snow lay round about, deep and crisp and even . . ."' I'm still singing as I head back into my apartment to get the rest of Trevor's accessories – a tweed cap for his head, and giant buttons for his eyes, mouth and coat. I go back outside and decorate him.

'There's something missing.'

I'm talking to myself, rather loudly.

'I know! Arms!'

I walk to the edge of the garden where the shrubbery meets the trees and pick up two long twigs. I push them into Trevor's sides and stand back to admire my handiwork. He's finished. Time for photographs!

I slide my phone out of my pocket and take about a dozen pictures, close-ups of Trevor's great parsnip nose, and wide shots of the garden to demonstrate his impressive height. In seconds, they are on Facebook.

'Meet Trevor, the tallest snowman in the land!'

Almost immediately, a friend comments: 'You built that yourself? You crazy girl!'

Crazy. Ha! Haha! I love it!

Mrs Spencer pops her head out again.

'Sharon, would you not come in? I've made some hot tea for you.'

'Fantabulous! Thank you. He's finished. I'll be in in just a tick.'

My neighbour puts her hand to her head, murmuring to herself. I take a last long look at my creation, clap my hands together loudly, then turn and follow her indoors.

* * *

Later that evening, my phone vibrates in my pocket. I ignore it. Who's disturbing me at this time of night?

'Ahh, what a perfect view!'

The vibrations start again. Maybe someone is in trouble. I answer this time.

'Hello?'

'Sharon, it's Lesley. I've been trying your landline. Where are you?'

'Just down by the Lagan. The river is so beautiful tonight. So many reflections! There are patches of ice, you know. It could really freeze tonight. Just think – we could go skating!'

'Sharon, you're talking too fast. How the heck did you get down there?'

'I walked.'

'From your apartment? In the snow? But that's miles!'

'I know! It was wonderful. Just me on the verge by the M3, hardly a car in sight.'

'How are you going to get home? You must be so cold.'

'Oh no, not at all. I'll just go back the way I came . . .'

'Sharon, I don't think you're well.'

'Oh, Lesley, I'm more than well. I love this weather! I'm better than I've ever been!'

'Huh. When are you seeing your doctor again?'

'Dr Harris? She's been on holiday, but I have an appointment on Friday. I can't wait to tell her how fantastically I am doing!'

'Right. Okay, this is ridiculous. It's 10 pm. I'm calling a taxi to get you home before they all quit.'

'There's no need . . .'

'Listen to me, Sharon. You're not well. I'm going to hang up and call Fonacab now. Where exactly are you?'

'At the weir, near the arena. Honestly, I wish you were here. It's so pretty.'

'Okay, okay. Now promise me you'll stay put until the taxi comes. Please!'

'No need to panic! I'll wait for the cab.'

'Good. I'm going to call round tomorrow. Try to get some sleep, okay?'

'Sure. I'll be a little angel. Sound asleep. Sleep like a baby.'

Lesley's sigh is audible. I laugh.

'Alright, bye.'

'Goodby-ee!'

'Now wait for that taxi!'

'Cheery-bye.'

* * *

The doorbell rings at eleven the next morning and I let Lesley in.

'Sharon! What are you wearing? Or rather, not wearing?!'

'I was cleaning. I got overheated so I took off my top.'

'So I gather. One of your neighbours could walk past your window. Do you really want them to see your bra?'

I shrug. I don't really care, but I pull on my jumper.

Lesley nods.

'That's better.'

'Isn't this place looking a million dollars? I've been up since five and I've done every room. Sparkling clean! I love sparkle. Do you want a coffee? The kettle's boiled!'

'Uh, I'm not sure you should be drinking coffee . . .'

'Coffee is great. Coffee makes the world go round. Coffee is fuel for the soul!'

'Ok-a-ay . . . I brought some scones. Freshly baked, with white chocolate – your favourite.'

'Oh, I'm not hungry. I don't need any food. My battery is fully charged, you see.'

'Your battery? Sharon, I'm so glad you're seeing your psychiatrist tomorrow. Something is really wrong.'

'Wrong? Extremely right, I would say. But I've missed Dr Harris. It will be good to see her. She'll be over-the-moon pleased with me.'

I bring the cafetière from the kitchen through to the dining table and plunge it immediately. I'm not in the mood for waiting around. I pour a cup for Lesley and another for me.

'I'm so excited about Iceland!'

'Iceland? What do you mean?'

'My holiday! I'm going next week. I booked on Monday. It's part of my new challenge. I'm going to swim in every geyser in the world! And hot springs too. I want to go to Budapest, but I have no money left.'

'Sharon, you can't go away like this! You're not well. And what do you mean you've no money left? How much did this trip to Iceland cost?'

'Of course I can go. It's going to be super-fab! And it was a bargain – £278 for three nights. It's the money I gave to the church that's the problem.'

'You gave money to the church?'

'Yes! I felt a calling. One thousand pounds for the new building. They're having counselling rooms, you know – I think it's really going to help people. I wrote to James and Kate and told them I want to bless them abundantly . . .'

'And now you have no money?'

'I used up my overdraft.'

'Your overdraft?! What have you been spending it all on?'

'We-ell, there was the melodica I wanted to learn, and the two whistles – they're top-of-the-range – and the colour printer for my computer, and . . .'

'Sharon, we're going to have to talk to James and Kate. You can't afford to just give like that.'

'But I am here on a special mission. I know I am. The Lord will provide.'

I take a long drink of my coffee.

'Mmm. That's so good.'

Lesley rolls her eyes.

'What else have you been doing?'

'Let's see. Oh yes! I've applied for a new job – I passed the online test. With my intellect, I can do anything I put my mind to! Did you know I have Grade 8 piano? And four As in my A levels. Sixty take thirty-five equals twenty-five. See? Maths! "I wandered lonely as a cloud . . ." See? English! *Je suis la plus belle* – that's French, right? Ha!'

Lesley slumps back in her chair.

'Are you going to be okay until tomorrow? Can I trust you just to stay here and keep out of trouble?'

'Trouble? I'm fine. Finer than fine. Fine wine.'

'Tell you what, I'll bring over my marking and do it here this afternoon.'

'Okay. We can work together. I'm writing my book; you can mark. Perfect!'

* * *

I arrive just in time for my usual 8.30 am appointment with Dr Harris. I'm wearing a miniskirt and boots and I have done my hair like Princess Leia.

'Sharon?'

Dr Harris squints at me, then turns, and I follow her to her office, humming something from *West Side Story*.

I take my usual seat, then stand up, spin round twice, swinging my arms, and sit down again.

Dr Harris clears her throat.

'It's been a few weeks. How have you been?'

'I've been brilliant! Better than ever in my whole life. Honestly, I have never felt so great! How are you, Dr Harris? Did you have a good holiday?'

'Mmm . . . yes, uh, thank you. What have you been doing since I last saw you? I think that was the first week in January.'

'I've been working on my novel. I've got eighty thousand words already.'

'Eighty thousand words? When did you start it?'

'Two weeks ago! I've been working night and day. It's about this girl called Ciara and she's a community worker in Galway, but she gets pregnant and she doesn't know how, but it's not an immaculate conception – it's just that she has a mental illness like me and she went into some fugue state where she didn't know what she was doing and a man had sex with her and now she doesn't know what to do, and she falls and breaks her leg and it's really dangerous for the baby . . .'

I stop amid a fit of coughing.

'That's a chesty cough you have there.'

'Well, you see, I was out in the snow a lot. Mrs Spencer said I would get pneumonia. That was the night I built Trevor. Trevor's my seven-foot snowman. He's in the garden at our apartments. I think he could marry people, like Parson Brown. And then on Wednesday I walked to the Lagan, but that wasn't too cold for long because Lesley got the taxi to bring me back and . . .'

'Sharon, slow down a minute.'

I cough again.

'I can't! I'm on superfuel. I haven't eaten since Tuesday. I don't need to. I'm the Duracell Bunny! Bunny, funny, right on the money!'

Dr Harris sits forward and leans her elbows on her desk. Her eyes are wider than usual and she's crinkling her nose. She takes a deep breath and clasps her hands together. I stand up and spin round again.

'Sharon, you're bipolar!'

'Really?'

'You're high as a kite. I wondered before, but . . . Definitely now.'

She combs her fingers through her thick red hair. I dissolve into a fit of giggles, almost falling off my chair.

What is bipolar disorder?

Bipolar disorder, also known as manic-depressive illness, is a brain disorder that causes unusual shifts in mood, energy, activity levels, and the ability to carry out day-to-day tasks.[2]

Bipolar disorder is a serious mental illness which endures throughout a person's lifetime. It is characterized by episodes of very high – 'manic' or 'hypomanic' – or very low (depressed) moods lasting for weeks or months, separated by periods of relatively normal mood. These mood changes can be associated with psychosis (losing the sense of what is real and what is not), and make it very difficult to sustain usual patterns of work and social activity.

Bipolar disorder most commonly emerges between the ages of 15 and 19, though it can take time to verify the diagnosis. It affects approximately 1% of the population and is a significant cause of disability worldwide.[3]

There is a strong genetic component to bipolar disorder, and it is associated with physical abnormalities of the brain's systems for controlling mood, but there is also an environmental component – stress and physical illness can provoke 'ups' and 'downs'.

The average life expectancy in bipolar disorder is between eight and a half and nine years shorter than that of the general population.[4] This is only partly owing to suicide rates. People with bipolar illness also suffer a greater frequency of deaths from cardiovascular disease, diabetes, chronic obstructive pulmonary disease and infections such as flu and pneumonia, as well as unintentional injuries.[5]

Even with these limitations and risks, people with bipolar disorder can live meaningful lives, as there are effective treatments available, both for the acute phases of the illness and to reduce the risk of relapse.

'Do you understand that you're not well?'

'I do feel – uh – different, but I have so much energy!'

'That's because you're manic. We have to bring you down again.'

'But I'm going to Iceland next week. I want to get my novel finished before then!'

'Iceland? Sharon, you are going nowhere. If I think you're getting on a plane to Iceland, I'll have to detain you in hospital. Do you want to go into the ward anyway? It might be easier . . .'

'No! I don't feel sick. I don't need the ward. I'm absolute-olutely grand at home.'

'Well, you're going to have to work with me, then. You have bipolar disorder. It's not a joke.'

I stifle a laugh and cough again.

'I'm going to prescribe a strong antipsychotic to bring you back down again, and we'll get you started on lithium as maintenance to stabilize your mood. Can you agree to take them?'

I swallow. She's taking this very seriously.

'Ye-es.'

'Well, I'm going to give you a note for your GP and I'm going to ring her myself. I need you to start these meds today, especially the antipsychotic. And I want her to see you if she can. You sound to me like you could do with an antibiotic as well.'

I spin again, arms in the air, then sit down and lean forward, earnest.

'Sharon, I need to see you again on Monday. We have to make sure this is going the right way. Listen, who did you book your flights to Iceland with? I think I should phone them and make sure you don't head off into the sunset!'

'It was a *Belfast Telegraph* deal. Aw, Dr Harris, I was so excited about it.'

'I know. But you have to understand that you may feel wonderful, but it won't last. You're really ill, but these new tablets will help. If you take them!'

'I'll take them.'

Somehow the gravity of the situation is hitting home. I wipe my brow.

'I want you to stay at home over the weekend. Can anyone be with you?'

'My friend Lesley – she's been really concerned – she might come round.'

'Good. Right, excuse me a second while I ring Dr Oates.'

She goes outside, but I can hear her on the phone to my GP. They are friends and talk on their mobiles without having to go through the surgery switchboard.

A few minutes later, she comes back in.

'Two-thirty. She'll see you before the afternoon surgery. Can I trust you to get there on time?'

I nod. Dr Harris shakes her head.

'Dr Oates always thought you had bipolar, you know.'

'Dr Oates is great.'

'She is. Right, I'm going to call a taxi to get you home. You're not walking to the bus in this weather with that chest.'

'Okay. Thanks, Dr Harris.'

'Sit in the waiting room – if you can sit. The hospital uses Value Cabs. They're usually not long in coming.'

'Thanks, Dr Harris.'

Bipolar. Hmm. How exciting!

What is mania?

Mania refers to elevated mood and is the defining symptom of bipolar disorder. An episode of mania lasts for at least one week and may go on indefinitely if untreated. It disrupts someone's ability to perform day-to-day activities, can be detrimental to relationships and often needs to be managed in hospital. The symptoms of mania involve a person's thinking, emotions and physical being.[6] They include, in order of mild to severe:

- Enhanced sense of well-being
- Excessive energy
- Feeling sociable and becoming more outgoing
- Having lots of new and exciting ideas
- A reduced need for food, or sometimes an increased appetite
- Needing less sleep
- Agitation – fidgeting or pacing
- Increased sexual desire
- Euphoria, uncontrolled excitement and excessive optimism
- Increased creativity, which increases productivity at first and then becomes chaotic

- Becoming distracted; poor concentration
- Racing, jumbled-up thoughts
- Rapid speech which jumps from one idea to another
- Experiencing changes in perception – sounds seem louder and colours are brighter
- Getting frustrated, impatient, irritable and angry
- Having 'delusions of grandeur' (see 'Mania and psychosis' below)

Mania also affects a person's behaviour. He or she may (going from mild to severe symptoms):

- Talk and/or write a lot
- Dress more flamboyantly
- Sign up for activities and take on new responsibilities
- Become the 'life and soul of the party'
- Make lots of jokes, witty or sarcastic remarks, and puns
- Behave inappropriately – for example, being overfamiliar to bosses at work
- Do things that are out of character
- Take more risks, including risks to personal safety
- Become sexually disinhibited
- Make ill-advised decisions, sometimes with terrible consequences
- Spend excessively
- Be rude, angry or aggressive
- Misuse drugs and alcohol, even if he or she normally doesn't drink
- Fail to take care of his or her physical needs

Hypomania is similar to mania but is less severe. A person who is hypomanic will experience most of the symptoms of mania, but to a lesser degree (so there are unlikely to be long-term consequences). The person is likely to be elated, energized and restless, but will not have delusions or fail to care for his or her physical needs.[7]

Mania and psychosis

Mania can also be coupled with psychosis (a detachment from reality), with hallucinations (which may be visual or involve hearing voices) and with delusions. The delusions are usually grandiose and consistent with the person's elevated mood. For example, the person may believe that they are invincible and have supernatural powers. This can lead to risk-taking behaviour, such as jumping off a building because the manic person thinks he or she can fly. People with mania often feel that they are on a special mission.

People who are manic and psychotic lose insight and do not realize that they are unwell, so they often get frustrated by attempts to help them.

A few hours later, my name appears in lights in Dr Oates's waiting room and I knock on her door.

'Well, Sharon, imagine that! A consultant psychiatrist backs up what I've said all along. You have bipolar disorder. Now we can get you on the right treatments and you should be better than you've ever been.'

'I'm already better than I've ever been! On top of the world looking down at creation!'

'Do you realize that you are ill?'

'I – I guess. I know things are going very fast. And I can't stay still.'

'Well, these drugs will help. We'll have to get you on to the lithium-level monitoring programme. You know we have to check your bloods every week or so, don't you?'

I nod. I learnt all about that in medical school.

'Now let me sound that chest . . . Deep breaths for me.'

I pull up my shirt for her.

'Yep, all the signs of a nasty infection. I'm going to start you on amoxicillin. It shouldn't interfere with your other drugs. Listen, I want to go home with you and look after you myself, but I can't. So you'll have to look after yourself.'

'I'll be good.'

My smile is broad.

'Okay, just like Dr Harris said – a quiet weekend at home, no outings in the cold. Just take your tablets, have something to eat and take plenty of hot drinks. You'll see her on Monday morning and I'm going to see you on Tuesday at eleven. Can you work with us?'

'Yes.'

'Because if you can't, it'll be back to the hospital!'

'I understand.'

'Call the out-of-hours GP any time, okay?'

'I don't think I'll need to.'

'Good, but if there's anything . . . just don't hesitate, right?'

I nod. I love Dr Oates. I know she really cares about me and I want to please her.

How is bipolar disorder treated?

Medication

Mood stabilizers are the backbone of treatment,[8] helping to stop someone's mood from going either too high or too low. Lithium is probably the best known and most commonly used, but anti-epileptic drugs and some antipsychotics can also be effective. Some patients need a combination of mood stabilizers to stay well.

Mania or hypomania is managed using **antipsychotics** and **tranquillizers**, which are usually stopped once the person's mood has returned to normal. Bipolar depression is harder to treat. **Antidepressants** are sometimes used, but these can sometimes trigger a manic episode; this risk is reduced if the patient is taking a mood stabilizer at the same time.[9]

Psychological treatments

Medication is most effective in bipolar disorder if it is combined with other treatments.[10] **Psycho-education** classes teach people about their condition and how to manage it themselves as well as they can, by monitoring their mood; regulating their routine; and balancing physical activity, social activities and rest. **Cognitive behavioural therapy** may help someone who has depressive symptoms and anxiety. A **clinical psychologist** may help the person to understand some of the environmental triggers for the illness, address underlying issues or teach coping skills.

Two weeks later and I am starting to come down. I lie on my sofa in the afternoon for the first time in more than a month. I've finished my novel, but I'm starting to wonder if it all makes sense, and Trevor is slowly melting in the garden. I'm concerned about my bank balance and worried about some of the text messages I have sent while I've been manic. And I'm on my third course of antibiotics for a chest infection that isn't shifting. Dr Harris was right – this bipolar thing really is serious.

Over time, my physical health improves, my blood tests show that my lithium levels are becoming consistent within the 'therapeutic range', and Dr Harris – who is seeing me twice every week now – is able to reduce the antipsychotic from the maximum 20 mg to the maintenance dose of 10 mg. I am eating again and sleeping a bit more at night, and my speech is more intelligible.

* * *

A couple of months later, I start working as a volunteer receptionist in my local constituency office, and life feels as though it has a purpose. Maybe this new diagnosis – scary as it is – will actually help me. It's weird telling my new boss in the office that I have bipolar disorder and that is why I am not working as a doctor. But I can recognize that I experienced milder manic, or hypomanic, episodes even in my early medical school career – and somehow the 'bipolar' label validates some of my suffering over the past few years.

Dr Oates says that bipolar depressive episodes can be different from those in major depressive disorder, and that might be why I haven't really responded to conventional antidepressants. There's even an association between bipolar disorder and problematic eating behaviour.

Yes, this really makes sense. Can I dare to hope that things might get better now?

11

Support for my application
Wrestling with the General Medical Council

Edinburgh is as cold, wet and grey – even on this spring day – as I have always imagined it. I have travelled on my own and I feel as though that in itself is a marker of my health. There is time for a coffee on Princess Street before my appointment, but I can hardly swallow it. My legs are jelly and my hands shake. I have to prove myself. I have to realize my dream.

A year has passed and I am well. Truly well. I have a diagnosis of a so-called 'severe and enduring mental illness' – bipolar disorder – but it means that I'm now getting the right medication. I am stable enough to work regularly in a voluntary role; I am enjoying Advanced French evening classes, meeting new people and also praying, reading my Bible and going to church. There are blips here and there, but overall, things are really positive. I can finally say I have hope for the future.

With Dr Harris's blessing, I have applied to the General Medical Council again for an assessment of my 'fitness to practise' medicine. This time they haven't rejected me outright but have invited me to attend two assessments with independent psychiatrists on dates six weeks apart, the first in Edinburgh, the second in Northern Ireland.

Dr Field's private practice is located in a tall Victorian terrace, which, according to the plaque at the door, is also home to a sleep medicine clinic. Interesting. I ring the bell and a receptionist shows me into a waiting room. I straighten my business suit and check my hair in a compact mirror.

It is exactly noon when I am summoned to the psychiatrist's consulting room.

Dr Field stands up from his leather-upholstered chair to greet me with a warm handshake.

'Sharon, do come in. Take a seat. You are most welcome.'

He is probably quite close to retirement age, broad-shouldered and swarthy, and his office is the epitome of tidiness and good taste. Neatly ordered files line shelves on one wall; medical journals line another. There is a large glass-and-mahogany coffee table in the middle of the room with a range of high-end lifestyle magazines fanned out on it, and two paintings of what I imagine to be the Scottish Highlands hang alongside the doctor's credentials behind his desk.

I sit down carefully.

'Now, we're here about fitness to practise, but I don't want you to worry too much about that. It will be much easier if we chat generally and I get to know you a little.'

He smiles and his eyes are gentle. I nod, my mouth dry.

'So, tell me about yourself.'

I put my hands on my knees so that their shaking is less obvious.

'Well, I'm twenty-eight. I live in Belfast. I graduated from medical school in 2007 but I wasn't fit to practise because of my bipolar disorder. Now I work in my local MP's constituency office. I mean, it's voluntary, but I'm getting lots of opportunities to use my skills.'

'That sounds very interesting. What sort of things do you do?'

'Well, it's not unlike a GP surgery. You never quite know what problem is going to come in next. And regardless of what it is, you have to use your initiative to address it.'

I am getting into my stride. I like talking about my work.

'Like, there are some things that are easy – someone's bins haven't been emptied this week, or they need help to fill out an application for housing benefit. But some things are a bit more challenging, like neighbourhood disputes where no one can see any but their own point of view. And you get some odd enquiries, like someone's washing machine isn't working and they want to know whether they should call an electrician or a plumber!'

'And you work in a good team?'

'Yes, there's just the constituency manager, a senior caseworker and me. My title is constituency support officer. I am still an unpaid intern, but they treat me as a regular member of staff and we all bounce ideas off each other.'

'It sounds like you really enjoy it.'

'I do.'

'And how long have you been there?'

'Just over a year now.'

'It sounds as though your health has been quite stable recently.'

'Yes. Ever since I started on the lithium and the olanzapine, I've done well. You see, before that they didn't know I had bipolar disorder so I didn't have a mood stabilizer, and there were a lot of ups and downs – particularly downs.'

'Indeed. Did you know that, on average, it takes about ten years from the first emergence of symptoms to a firm diagnosis of bipolar disorder?'

'No, but that's interesting, because that was almost exactly the time frame for me.'

'And it's unfortunate, because bipolar disorder is eminently treatable. You may not be aware of this, but there are a lot of doctors who have a diagnosis of bipolar. It certainly does not preclude clinical practice.'

I feel the muscles in my neck becoming less taut.

'Do you enjoy anything in particular outside of work?'

'Yes. I've been taking an evening class in French for an Advanced Diploma. I love languages and I have a French friend who does conversation classes with me in Starbucks every other Tuesday.'

'That sounds challenging.'

'The good thing about a language class is that you hear people's opinions as you discuss different topics, and you get to know them quite quickly.'

'So, you have good friends around you?'

'Yes. I mean, not just in my French class. I have some good friends who live near me and go to my church, and I'm still in touch with classmates from school and medical school.'

'It sounds as though you are living quite a full life.'

'Yes, it's been so much better with the new medication.'

'And you seem to have a good rapport with your psychiatrist. That comes through in the paperwork the GMC sent me.'

'Dr Harris has been great. She sees me less often now, but I have really come a long way under her care.'

'I'm glad to hear it.'

I loosen the grip of my hands on my knees. They still tremble, but less visibly.

'Let's talk about your medication. You're taking lithium?'

'Yes. My levels are quite stable now.'

'Well, that is the gold standard treatment for your condition. Does it give you any side effects?'

'My skin. I used to have really clear skin, and now, as you see . . .'

I shake my head. I can feel my neck flush.

'That could be hard for you.'

'Yes, but my doctors say that acne is the lesser evil.'

'There's probably truth in that. Do you notice anything else – sleepiness, perhaps?'

'Yes. Everyone says that lithium isn't a sedative, but I find that it is. I can focus okay in work in the mornings, but sometimes I fall asleep in the cinema or just on my sofa in the evenings. And I don't think it's just the olanzapine, though that probably doesn't help.'

'I believe you. Do you know, I once took part in a clinical trial of lithium as a control? I was supposed to take it at a therapeutic dose for six weeks, but I had to quit after three because I simply couldn't work. It was like thinking through cement.'

I smile. 'Exactly.'

'But I understand that people do function at a high level while taking lithium, and again I wouldn't be thinking, "This person is on lithium: they can't be a doctor."'

I am grateful for Dr Field's openness. We talk a bit about my previous history, but he is definitely more interested in how I am now, and he seems content with everything I tell him.

'Well, Sharon, it's been a pleasure meeting you. Thank you for making the journey on this awful day.'

'It's been a pleasure meeting you too, Dr Field.'

'I will be writing a report for the GMC within the next fortnight. I gather that you have another assessor to see?'

'Yes, at the end of next month.'

'They probably won't give you my report until both have been submitted, but I am happy to tell you that I will be supporting your application. You have been articulate and honest, and I don't see why you couldn't be using your problem-solving skills in a medical setting rather than the constituency office.'

I bite my lip, trying not to betray just how excited this makes me feel. 'Thank you so much.'

'Thank you. I wish you every success. Safe home, now.'

'Goodbye.'

'Goodbye.'

I get drenched as I make my way to the airport shuttle, but nothing could dampen my spirits. Perhaps I am going to be a doctor after all.

12

The network in
the fourth dimension
Wrestling with psychosis

There's something wrong. Dr Harris has changed roles and I sit down in the corner of her big new office at the psychiatric hospital just outside the city. I've been here once before, but today is different. Long fingers of darkness creep towards me from the walls and I can sense an evil presence behind my left shoulder.

'Sharon? Why are you cowering over there? Come and take a seat here.'

I don't move.

'Okay, then, stay there if you prefer. How are you doing?'

'Fine.' I speak quickly and quietly.

'You've been to see the GMC assessor since I saw you. Dr Field, wasn't it? How did that go?'

'Fine.'

'You felt it went well?'

'It was okay.'

'You're not very forthcoming today, Sharon. Are you okay?'

'I'm fine.'

'Something's not right. Tell me what's going on for you.'

'I can't talk. It's the conspiracy. This place might be bugged.'

'The conspiracy? What conspiracy?'

'It's in the fourth dimension. Messages are travelling through the network. You're involved, but you don't know it.'

'I'm definitely not involved in a conspiracy, Sharon. I haven't heard you speak of this before. What's this fourth dimension?'

I turn and cast a quick glance over my left shoulder. I shudder.

'What are you looking at?'

'Nothing.'

'Something in the fourth dimension?'

I bow my head slowly, press my hand to my right temple. The darkness is starting to consume the office space. I look at Dr Harris and her face contorts.

'Are you really not going to talk to me today?'

'I can't.'

'Because this room is bugged?'

'Yes.'

'And who do you think has bugged it?'

'The co-conspirators.'

'What are these conspirators trying to do?'

I curl my shoulders in and hug my knees.

'Sharon? You're really not going to talk?'

I shake my head.

'When is your next GMC assessment?'

'Next Friday.'

'Hmm. I think we might have to try something. You've never been on chlorpromazine, have you?'

'No.'

'Well, here's a note for Dr Oates. I just want you to try this small dose. It might help with some of these – uh – strange thoughts. Will you take it for me?'

I pause for a second.

'Will you?'

'Yes.'

'I can't hear you.'

'Yes.'

'Okay, here it is then. I can't see you again until after your assessment, unfortunately, but if you can come on the following Wednesday, same time, we'll see how you've got on. Right?'

I get up and reach for the note, careful not to meet her probing eyes, then move quickly towards the door.

'Goodbye, Sharon.'

I get a taxi directly to my GP surgery. The evil presence accompanies me. I hand in the note and the receptionist says she thinks the doctor is doing prescriptions at the moment and might be able to write this for me now.

A few minutes later, she returns with a green slip. Chlorpromazine, 25 mg. I take it to the pharmacy next door.

I go home and take the tiny round tablet, then set out on a walk around a few of the streets nearby, delivering invitations to a community meeting organized by the constituency office.

Oh. Oh dear. I put my hand to my heart. Just a few skipped beats. I walk on. Just this next street to do. I try to walk up the hill but my legs weaken and I can feel the colour drain from my face. I lean against a gatepost. More skipped beats, then constant fluttering. I stagger forward a few steps. My strength starts to return, then fades again. I feel sick. The world is closing in. Someone help me, please.

Thankfully, my delivery route has taken me close to my GP surgery again. I wobble my way back there, stopping and starting, catching my breath, losing my balance, all the while my heart fluttering.

I'm holding my chest when I arrive. The receptionist says she'll call the duty doctor straight away, and in seconds Dr Oates emerges from the corridor and checks my pulse.

'Sharon, we need to get you lying down.'

She takes my arm and walks me into the treatment room. She addresses the nurses loudly.

'This girl needs an ECG immediately.'

I lie down on the narrow bed, but it doesn't help me feel any better.

'Your pulse is 160 and irregular. Did you take the chlorpromazine?'

'Yes.'

'Then I think this is probably a drug reaction. We're going to have to get you to A&E.'

'No, please!'

'I know, pet. You hate it. But you have to go, okay? We need you on a heart monitor.'

I hear her calling for an ambulance. Things become blurry. I'm on the verge of losing consciousness.

Dr Oates stays with me until my transport arrives. I feel hot tears on my cheeks.

'You're gonna be okay, love. It'll probably just settle with time, but we have to make sure.'

She's right. Over the next few hours, the monitor in the Accident and Emergency Department shows my heart rate settling and the beats regaining their regular pattern. The doctor there is kind.

'We're just going to keep you here overnight to be sure, but things are going the right way. Just don't take any more chlorpromazine. That was a very low dose to provoke such a significant reaction.'

* * *

Dr Toal shows me into his small office in the rural hospital.

'Take a seat.'

He motions to a warped plastic chair directly facing his desk, which is piled with blue folders. Patient files. The setting could not be more different from Dr Field's elegant private consulting room.

I haven't made eye contact yet. It's May, but I shiver, crouching in my seat.

'Now, we both know why you're here. I've been asked by the GMC to assess your fitness to practise.'

I twist my head to the right, looking away from the evil presence.

Dr Toal inclines his head, looking over his reading glasses.

'Are you okay? Do you need a drink or anything?'

'Yes. Er, no, thanks.'

'You seem nervous. That's understandable.'

'It's not – it's not the assessment. Just that . . . the tormentors. They're here.'

'Tormentors? Mm-hmm. Tell me about those.'

'They're grey like pterodactyls and they're flapping . . .'

I look up at the ceiling, first to one corner, then another. I make myself even smaller in my chair.

'And you can see these – these pterodactyls?'

'Yes.'

My voice is low.

Dr Toal lifts his pen and writes something on the pad in front of him.

'I gather your psychiatrist is Dr Harris. Does she know about the tormentors?'

'She's not my psychiatrist any more.'

'Oh? I still have her name here. Who are you seeing now?'

'No one.'

'So Dr Harris has discharged you?'

'No. I just can't go back.'

'Why not?'

'It's because of the conspiracy against me in the fourth dimension. Dr Harris is on the network. They're using her, but she doesn't know it. She tried to kill me. With chlorpromazine.'

Dr Toal takes off his glasses and raises his eyebrows.

'You think Dr Harris tried to kill you?'

'Her room is bugged. The co-conspirators have an entry point from the fourth dimension. I keep getting messages – on the network. They're like electric pulses.'

'Am I part of this network?'

'I don't know yet. It depends.'

I look up and to the right, then clasp my hands tightly, my face twitching.

'Sharon, do you think that you are well?'

He has set down his pen now and is leaning towards me.

'Ye-es. I mean – I'm tormented. The tormentors are here. And the evil presence. But there's nothing wrong with me. It's just that I have been chosen by God to be tortured. That's all.'

'Chosen by God to be tortured. Okay.'

He pulls his chair in closer to his desk.

'Sharon, I don't think we need to take this any further today. You're quite distressed.'

I raise my shoulders to my ears, eyes darting around the room.

'How did you get here?'

'My friend brought me.'

'And is your friend taking you home again?'

'Yes.'

'That's good. Do you drive, Sharon?'

'Yes.'

'Well, I don't think you should be driving for now. Do you understand? You're – uh – distracted.'

I nod.

'I'm going to do my report, but I'm also going to write to your GP. That's still Dr Oates?'

'Yes.'

'Okay, Sharon. I'll just see you out.'

'Thanks.'

'Thank you.'

* * *

On Monday morning, a letter arrives for me in the mail.

Dear Dr Oates,

cc. Dr K. Harris, Dr S. McConville

Re: GMC Fitness to Practise Assessment:
Dr Sharon McConville

I assessed Dr McConville today, Friday 27 May, as requested by the General Medical Council. I found her to be floridly psychotic, apparently experiencing visual and auditory hallucinations involving 'tormentors' in a 'fourth dimension'.

I am concerned that she seems to have disengaged from her psychiatrist, Dr Harris, whom she believes is involved in a plot to kill her. It is my view that she needs to be seen urgently by psychiatric services, with a view to reviewing her anti-psychotic regimen.

I would be grateful for your action in this regard.

Yours sincerely,

Dr H. Toal

What is psychosis?

Psychosis is characterized as disruptions to a person's thoughts and perceptions that make it difficult for them to recognize what is real and what isn't.[1]

A person suffering from psychosis will typically have hallucinations and/or delusions.

A **hallucination** is the perception of something – a sound, vision, smell or taste – that is not real and is not perceived by anyone else. Many people with psychosis hear voices, which can be friendly, but are usually unpleasant, derogatory or mocking in character. The voices are very real to the person who hears them: on certain types of brain scan, the same areas that light up when a person speaks are illuminated when the person hears voices.[2]

Delusions are 'fixed false beliefs or suspicions not shared by others in the person's culture and that are firmly held even when there is evidence to the contrary'.[3] Someone who has a delusion will often have 'worked-out' reasons why the belief is true, but these reasons don't make sense to anyone else. Someone may have a paranoid delusion that his or her house is wired, or may be deluded about his or her own identity, thinking that he or she is the Queen or the Messiah.

People with psychosis may feel as if their thoughts or their bodies are being **controlled**. It may seem as though someone is 'stopping' their thoughts mid-flow, stealing thoughts from their mind or inserting unwanted thoughts into their brain. People often try to find explanations for these frightening symptoms, such as that someone is targeting them with controlling 'laser beams' or that an evil force is taking them over.

Dr Oates rings me at lunchtime.

'Did you get a letter from Dr Toal this morning?'

'Yes.'

'Did it make any sense to you?'

'I guess.'

'Sharon, I'm concerned about you too. I'm going to refer you to the Home Treatment Team for assessment. If you won't see Dr Harris, you'll have to see somebody else.'

'Yes.'

'I'm on your side, okay? We're going to get this sorted.'

'Thanks.'

* * *

The following week, a white A4 envelope arrives, but I already know what the outcome is going to be.

The cover letter is short.

Dear Dr McConville,

We regret to inform you that we have assessed your case and found that you are unfit to practise. We cannot offer GMC registration at this time.

Please find enclosed reports from Dr J. Field and Dr H. Toal. You will note that, while Dr Field writes in support of your application, Dr Toal raises concerns and is unable to support it.

The GMC requires that both independent assessors must be in agreement before we can declare a doctor fit to practise.

We advise that you seek to establish a more prolonged period of stability with regard to your mental health before you make any further application . . .

I file the reports in my cabinet without looking at them. I am less devastated than I was at the first rejection. I am beginning to recognize that I am not well.

The following afternoon, the Home Treatment Team admits me to hospital urgently.

* * *

I pace the corridors of the ward, which form a square. I complete circuit after anxious circuit, half shuffling, my tracksuit bottoms dragging on the floor. I wring my hands, fighting back tears, looking at the floor, avoiding the concerned eyes of nurses and any possible interaction with other patients.

My key nurse, Claire, stops me close to my tiny bedroom.

'Do you want to come in here for a chat before the doctor sees you?'

I give my silent assent by opening my door for her. We sit on the bed.

'How are you feeling?'

I shake my head.

'Dr Rogers might want to change your medication. I think he has a few things to discuss with you – about the symptoms you've been having, you know? Do you feel like you can talk to him?'

'Will you come with me?'

'Of course.'

How is psychosis treated?

The mainstay of treatment is antipsychotic medication, which can reduce the intensity and frequency of delusions and hallucinations, lead to improvements in thinking and help with motivation and independent self-care.[4] It is usually given in tablet form, but if someone finds it difficult to manage medication or feels ambivalent about taking it, an antipsychotic may be given by injection every few weeks by a community psychiatric nurse.

Antipsychotic medication can have side effects – such as weight gain and sedation – and sometimes causes more serious complications, so it is important that the physical health of people with psychotic illness is carefully monitored.

There is a knock on the door and I can see one of the nursing assistants looking at me through the little tinted pane of glass. The psychiatrist is ready. I've only met this one once, on my last admission, and I know he tends to get straight to the point.

My right eye twitches. I pull my hair so that it half covers my face. I don't really want him to look at me. My mind is transparent. He might see more than I want to reveal.

As I walk up the corridor, the tormentors follow me, flying to my left this time. Their shadowy wings flap, their pointed heads diving in and out towards me and away again, sending coded messages right to the core of my brain. They laugh, mocking me. I pause and lean against the opposite wall for a second.

'Are they there again?'

I nod, my tired eyes pleading with the nurse for help.

'We'll tell the doctor about it now, sure. He'll know what to do.'

I breathe in sharply. Perhaps.

Claire opens a heavy green door to reveal a large room with two bay windows and a collection of sofas and orthopaedic chairs. Only Dr Rogers is there, my medical notes in his hand. The tormentors keep flapping just within my peripheral vision. In a moment of courage, I look towards them, then shudder, cowering away.

The doctor stands up and holds out his hand. I take it and we share a weak handshake.

'Take a seat, Sharon, please.'

He motions to a high beige chair set just apart from him and at an angle.

'I gather you met my trainee, Dr Scullion, last night. I've been reading her notes about what prompted your admission. Do you want to explain what happened?'

I look at my hands. 'It wasn't good.'

'So I gather. You were walking in the park and you were having thoughts of jumping off a bridge into traffic?'

I sit up straight and raise my hands to my head.

'I had to. Something was going on in the atmosphere and no one else knew. I was getting messages from the network – in the fourth dimension.'

'And you thought the only way to stop something really bad happening was for you to die – is that right?'

'Yes.'

'But you didn't do it.'

'I was scared.'

'You ran away instead.'

'Yes.' My face flushes red.

'I'm glad of that.'

There is a pause.

'Sharon, how is your mood?'

I shrug. 'It's okay.'

'You were very depressed on your last admission, but you're not really now?'

'No. I don't think so.'

'I don't think so either. I think the mood stabilizer and the new antidepressant are really working for you.'

I shiver, turning my head. The tormentors taunt me.

'But we're still having problems, aren't we?'

He flips my notes closed and looks up, catching my eye for the first time.

'I know we've all been working on the basis that you have bipolar disorder. By all accounts, you've certainly had your highs and lows.'

'Yes.'

'How would you feel if I told you that I think there's a bit more going on than that – that you have schizoaffective disorder?'

I look up. He starts explaining.

'It's a condition where you have bipolar symptoms, but even when your mood is – inverted commas – normal, you can still have psychotic symptoms. Sharon, these problems you're having – the "tormentors", the "network" – they are due to psychosis. They're not real, even though I know they're very real to you.'

That's for sure.

I lose concentration. Schizoaffective disorder. Schizoaffective disorder. I turn the words over in my head. I remember learning about it on my psychiatry attachment at medical school and also being told that I didn't need to know much – schizophrenia and bipolar disorder were much more common. I need to know now.

A voice in my head protests. But I'm not psychotic! But this really is real! People just don't understand because they're not privy to what I can see . . .

Or am I?

What is schizoaffective disorder?

Schizoaffective disorder has been defined as 'a chronic mental health condition characterized primarily by symptoms of schizophrenia, such as hallucinations or delusions, and symptoms of a mood disorder, such as mania and depression'.[5]

The 'schizo' prefix refers to symptoms of psychosis, while the term 'affect' in psychiatry refers to mood. Schizoaffective disorder is therefore a condition where there is a combination of symptoms involving problems with thinking and problems with mood.

It is less common than schizophrenia or bipolar disorder, with one study suggesting that 0.3% of the population are affected.[6] Because the condition is rarer than other severe mental illnesses, it has been less widely researched, so less is known about it. Most treatments used are based on those known to be effective in schizophrenia or bipolar disorder.

We do know that people with schizoaffective disorder have an imbalance in the neurotransmitter dopamine. Neuroscientists are also beginning to recognize structural differences in the brains of people with the condition. There is also a genetic component – people with schizoaffective disorder are more likely to have relatives with either schizoaffective disorder, bipolar disorder or schizophrenia.

Among the severe and enduring mental illnesses, schizoaffective disorder has the greatest impact on life expectancy, with female patients dying on average 17.5 years earlier than the general population.[7] Early deaths are frequently a result of natural causes, such as cardiovascular disease, but it is also thought that around 10% of people with schizoaffective disorder will die by suicide.

Dr Rogers has finished. Claire walks me back to my room. Why do I feel so tired? I lie on my back and stare at the ceiling. The tiny tiles blur into a moving ocean of grey. The evil presence is there again.

Claire leaves me to rest, but pops back in a few minutes later.

'I just wanted to let you know – the doctor has increased the dose of your antipsychotic. It's at the highest dose now, so he'll review it next week and maybe consider something else if we're not seeing an improvement. He doesn't want you to leave the ward for now. You'll understand why.'

Yes. I'm a suicide risk because I can't tell what's real and what's not. Schizoaffective disorder. Is that a final diagnosis? Depression, bipolar, EDNOS . . . and now this. Schizo. How I hate that term.

Myth-buster

People with schizophrenia or schizoaffective disorder are violent.

In news bulletins, when we hear about a violent crime, the first thing that is often mentioned about the perpetrator is that he or she 'has paranoid schizophrenia'. Sometimes this is inaccurate; sometimes it is irrelevant (if someone with diabetes commits a crime, their diagnosis is unlikely to be mentioned!).

It is true that a tiny minority of people with psychotic illness do commit acts of violence. Sometimes these are driven by paranoia, or by voices that command them to act in a certain way, but violent behaviour is especially rare in people whose condition is managed appropriately. People with psychosis are actually about fourteen times more likely to be the victims of crime than to perpetrate it, and are considerably more vulnerable to being victims than people who do not have psychosis.[8]

13

A complicated little creature
Wrestling, with fresh hope

Two months later, I am discharged home. I'm taking the maximum dose of my antipsychotic, and it makes me feel so nauseous that I have to swallow two different anti-sickness tablets and one stomach protector along with it. But it's working, and I'm no longer living in the fourth dimension.

I decide that I'm going to become as healthy as a person with schizoaffective disorder can be. My GP refers me to a scheme that offers free gym membership and personal fitness instruction to people with chronic illness. I love the endorphin rush that cardio and resistance training gives me, so much so that I am soon working out five times a week. It gets me up and out of my flat and makes me feel alive.

I also take up writing as a discipline – no more manic 'novel-in-two-weeks' scribbling, but regular journalling and attempts at some poetry and short stories. I find it therapeutic, and when I share bits and pieces of work with my friends, they seem to like them.

Two of my oldest friends, Esther and Lesley, support me steadily, quietly, lovingly. We have lots of heart-to-heart conversations over coffee in a little National Trust property close to where I live, and I feel as though I am valued by each of them as a friend, rather than just a 'project'.

Esther belongs to the church I went to as a student – the place of my baptism – and she is eager for me to go back. But I'm scared.

I feel so different now. I want to be accepted, but I said and did things in my psychotic moments that gave people good cause to alienate me.

'Trust me. People understand you've not been well. They'll give you another chance.'

'Maybe sometime soon. I'm just not ready.'

Esther and Lesley share a passion for Jesus that is infectious. Being around them makes me want to live out my faith. I struggle to read my Bible, but I get into the habit of rising at 6 am to spend an hour listening to Christian music and Googling images with verses that mean something to me, emblazoned against colourful pictures.

> Even the darkness will not be dark to you;
> the night will shine like the day,
> for darkness is as light to you.
> (Psalm 139:12)

> And the peace of God, which transcends all understanding,
> will guard your hearts and your minds in Christ Jesus.
> (Paul's letter to the Philippians 4:7)

In my new-found zeal, I start sharing these on social media. I want other people to know that God is speaking to me, even in the midst of my mental illness. That he is penetrating my darkness. That his peace is guarding my heart and mind.

And so I build a routine. Time with God before breakfast, down to the gym mid-morning, a phone call with my aunt Olivia every day after lunch, some writing in the afternoon, TV or more music in the evening. It's simple, but it's working.

There's a row of thirteen pill boxes on my kitchen shelf, but if that's what it takes to keep me well, I'm not going to complain.

December is cold, and I get chilled a few times waiting for the bus after the gym. I catch pneumonia just before Christmas and have to spend the day on my own. I'm exhausted, but I pass the time browsing the internet, looking for creative writing classes. I have determined that I'm going to improve my skills and meet some other writers in the new year. A Wednesday morning class running in a local arts centre catches my eye. I take the plunge and sign myself up.

I'm run down physically, but I'm ready to use my brain again. It's time for another new beginning. I might even go back to church.

* * *

There must be ten or eleven of us sitting at our desks, which form a U shape around the room. Great shafts of January sunlight blaze through the long windows. It's airy and clean and it feels like a good place to unleash some creativity.

Rebecca, our tutor, sits opposite us. She has fine mousey hair and wears a woollen dress.

'Welcome, everyone, to our creative writing class. I'm looking forward to getting to know you all. I think I recognize a few faces. Let's go around the room and share our names and the sort of writing we've been doing or would like to do.'

There's Seamus, who is working on a novel about boats; Samantha, who is a copywriter and longs to create something other than a blurb for washing powder; Lucy, who has had a few poems published; Emma, who keeps a journal but would like to try her hand at poetry . . .

I'm going last. I lose track as my turn approaches. My hands are clammy.

'I'm Sharon and I wrote my first novel last year, but it was a bit rushed. I'd like to get some feedback on my writing and maybe try some poetry.'

'Did you finish your novel?' Rebecca smiles and looks at me over the top of her glasses.

'Yes, I have a draft, but it would need a lot of work, and I'm not sure if I want to go back to it.'

'Still, it's a great achievement. Something to build on!'

The class murmur in agreement. I feel my cheeks redden.

The door opens and a head pops through.

'Ah, and you must be Robert.'

'Uh, yes. I'm sorry I'm late. The traffic . . .'

'Don't worry. Take a seat. We've just been getting to know each other and hearing about the sort of work we all want to do this term. You'll pick up the names as we go. Do you get called Robert or Rob?'

'Both. My friends call me Rob.'

Robert or Rob is probably a bit older than me, tall and bald, but with a brown beard. I notice that he has an unusually squiggly vein on the side of his forehead. He sits down and says that he is interested in writing science fiction.

Since no one has come prepared with work to discuss, Rebecca distributes a few samples of writing taken from three novels and a short story. We read them aloud together and discuss each author's 'voice'. Rebecca says that an important part of this term's class will be finding our own distinctive voices.

'It's easy to write like someone else, but I want to hear from you!'

Her expression broadens, and she looks at each of us in turn. I feel my heart beat a little faster.

'For next week, I want you to write a piece of "flash fiction". That's a very short story – just about two hundred to two hundred and fifty words – and I'm not going to set any limits to your imagination. Write about anything, but I want there to be an unexpected ending. Surprise us all!'

I feel cogs turning in my brain already. I thank Rebecca and smile at the other group members. I think I'm going to enjoy this class.

Downstairs in the café, I order an Americano and a bagel with butter and jam. It'll be a while before I get home.

I am sitting on a stool at a high table in the middle of the café when I sense someone just behind me. It's squiggly vein man from the class. Robert or Rob. I set my coffee down.

'Hi. Sharon, isn't it?'

'Yes. Hi . . . uh . . . Rob.'

'Do you mind if I join you?'

He's holding a large latte rather precariously.

'No. Sit down.'

He sets his coffee on the table and pulls out the other stool. He has a briefcase with him and he puts it carefully on the floor.

There is a moment of silence. I swish my long hair back over my shoulder.

'I – I was wondering if I had seen you at South Belfast Baptist Church on Sunday . . . '

I choke on a dry lump of bagel.

'Excuse me . . . Yes, I was there.'

'I recognized your coat.'

Oh yes. The coat of many colours which divides opinion among my friends.

'Do you go there often?'

'Pretty regularly in the evenings. There's a group of guys who usually hang out together after the service. Do you?'

'It was my first time back, to be honest. I used to be a regular, but . . . '

I feel my face reddening and turn away for a second.

'I'm glad it was you. It would have been a bit awkward if it wasn't!'

Rob smiles. His blue eyes are soft.

I've finished my bagel. He's still sipping his large latte.

'Are you heading home now?'

'Yes. I get a bus in town. It's easier than bringing the car – it's so hard to get parked.'

'I know! I'm heading into town too. Uh – do you want to walk down together?'

I button the infamous coat.

'Yes. That would be nice.'

Rob is so tall that he walks lopsidedly, leaning his ear towards me so that we can chat. There doesn't seem to be any shortage of things to talk about.

I learn that he's a freelance TV editor; I tell him that I was a doctor, but that I've been taking time out because of illness. I say 'bipolar' because he's more likely to understand that than 'schizoaffective disorder'. He confesses that he knows what it's like to be low. He's lost his mum to cancer and his dad died when he was little.

We pass the Ulster Hall. He slows for a second.

'Do you like music?'

'Yes. It's my therapy. I used to play in the Praise Group at the Baptist church, actually. Do you?'

'Oh yes. All kinds. Classical, rock, jazz.'

'You like classical?'

'Yes.'

'Well . . . there's a lunchtime concert at the Ulster Hall next Wednesday. It's at one, so I was thinking of going after class. It's Vivaldi, I think.'

'Would you like to go together?'

We've stopped walking and I'm looking up at him. 'Ye-es. Yes, that would be lovely.'

He wipes his brow.

'Oh, there's my bus! I'll have to go. But see you next week!'

'Yes, see you next week.'

He watches and waves as my bus pulls away from the stand.

I am smiling inside and out. I sigh through pursed lips. This is unexpected.

* * *

The following week, Rob walks me down to the concert hall after class. He is first to speak.

'I really liked your flash fiction.'

'Yours was great too. That post-apocalyptic landscape – you evoked it so well.'

'Thanks. But that bit at the end where the pen became a weapon – no one could have predicted that.'

'It was a bit gory, wasn't it?'

I giggle and pull my scarf up round my face.

There's a steady stream of folk entering the hall. A mixture of suited business people and civil servants on their lunch breaks and elderly people out for a day in the town.

Rob holds the doors for me, then guides me to a seat with a gentle hand at my back. He helps me off with my multicoloured coat and sets it on an empty chair for me. Warmth travels from my heart to my face.

'You're very chivalrous.'

Rob laughs quietly.

'Just looking after a lady.'

A lady. I sit up straight. Not just a mental case – a lady. But he doesn't really know me . . .

'Can you see past that pillar?'

'Oh yes, thanks.'

The members of the orchestra take their places. The music is beautiful and somehow the sound resonates with me more than usual. The programme lasts about forty minutes. People have to get back to work. It ends, and we applaud. Rob and I have no agenda.

I catch him trying to read my face. I beam at him.

'Did you enjoy that?'

'Yes. The strings were magnificent.'

'You like the strings?'

'Yes.'

'Me too.'

We look at each other, then down at our knees. He helps me back into my coat. 'Do you want to get some lunch?'

'Ye-es.' I shuffle from one foot to the other.

'It's okay if you have somewhere else to be . . .'

'No. Oh no, it's not that. I just – I just get a bit anxious about eating in front of people, that's all.'

'It's okay. I won't look! I'm hungry, so I'll be fully focused on my own plate!'

I laugh, twisting my hair around my index finger.

'There's a place just next door. I go there sometimes on a break from editing. It's good.'

He holds the doors for me again. I feel like I've gained two inches in height.

I eat awkwardly, but he's true to his word. We chat without focusing too much on our food. The concert, the morning's class and the various characters who were there, favourite authors, church, the cultural life of Belfast . . . we cover them all.

I look at the clock above the bar. It reads 4 pm.

'Goodness, is that the time?'

'Sorry, I've kept you back.'

'No, no. Not at all. It's been great – really great. But my friend Lesley is coming round this evening. I need to get home.'

'Of course. Is there a bus soon?'

'There's a bus every seven minutes.'

'That's handy . . . Uh, Sharon?'

'Yes?'

'There's a film on at Queen's Film Theatre on Friday night. *A Dangerous Method*. I was thinking of going . . .'

'Oh, I saw that in the programme. About Jung and Freud and psychotherapy? I thought it looked interesting too.'

'Would you like to come with me?'

I hesitate for a second, look up at him.

'Yes. I'd love to.'

He pulls a phone from his pocket.

'We ought to exchange numbers. Just in case.'

I can hear blood whooshing in my ears.

I give him my number and let him type his details into my contacts. Robert Hastings. Hastings. A distinguished, English-sounding name. I roll it around my mouth.

'Okay, great. I'll see you in the foyer before the film.'

I nod.

'What about meeting half an hour early? They serve good coffee.'

'Sure.'

His eyes are bright, his cheeks dimpling.

'See you then.'

'Yes, see you.'

On the bus I find it hard to regulate my breathing. It's so long since I've spent half a day with a man. It's so long since I've spent half a day with anyone. And to find so much in common! I slide down in my seat, cuddle my coat around me. Friday can't come soon enough.

* * *

Rob is a bit later than we agreed and I have a moment of panic, but I get myself a coffee and soon he appears, puffing and flustered.

'Sorry I'm late. I couldn't get parked.'

'It's okay. Here, sit down. Do you want me to get you a coffee?'

'That would be great.'

I notice that he's watching me as I wend my way back through the tables to the sofa that I grabbed for us at the back.

'You look really pretty tonight.'

I'm wearing a grey-and-purple shift dress, and I've put on some mascara, but not much else. I stiffen.

'Sorry. Did I say the wrong thing?'

'No, I mean . . . it's just . . .'

I pause, draw breath, start mumbling.

'I feel uncomfortable when people comment on my appearance. I used to have an eating disorder . . . I had to learn that appearances weren't important . . . Sorry, it's silly.'

'No, it's not silly. I just wanted to give you a compliment.'

'I know. Thanks.'

Rob leans back and laughs, shaking his head.

'What is it?'

'You're just a complicated little creature, aren't you?'

His good humour is infectious. I smile.

'Yes, I guess I am.'

I find the film utterly compelling, but there's quite a lot of 'adult' content and I squirm in my seat at times, wondering what this church-going guy is making of it. At least it was his suggestion. I sneak a few surreptitious glances at him and he doesn't seem too uncomfortable.

He sits on at the end, waiting to watch the credits.

'Sorry, I like to see where the editing was done.'

'Have you ever worked on a film?'

'No. Lots of music videos though. I edited and produced a music video in Israel once. I'll have to show it to you sometime.'

'I'd like that. I've never been to Israel.'

We get up and follow the crowd back out into the café.

'Well, did you like it?'

He cocks his head sideways. 'I thought it was really interesting. It made me think. I like something cerebral like that.'

'Me too . . . I was worried you might not like the – uh – sexual bits?'

'I guess when you go to a film and it's rated 15 you expect some of that. I did a master's in Film and TV production, so I've watched a lot of stuff. Maybe I'm a bit hardened. Were you okay with it?'

'I feel a bit guilty watching things like that sometimes, but I did think it was a really good film.'

We talk about the characterization, and the dynamics between Freud and Jung, and the fantastic locations, and Keira Knightley's performance.

'It's great to talk to someone who really understands film, Sharon.'

I hunch my shoulders up to my ears.

'I don't know if I really understand it all that well. I guess I just have some opinions and I don't normally get to share them with anyone.'

'Well, it's been good discussing it with you tonight.'

We walk towards the road where it turns out we've both left our cars. We get to his first. He drives a BMW. I think about my battered little Corsa and hope he doesn't see its big dent in the dark.

'Do you want to sit in for a second?'

'Uh . . . okay.'

He opens the passenger door for me and I climb in, then he walks round and swings into the driver's seat.

'You have a lovely car.'

'You like it?'

'Yes.'

We sit in silence for a moment or two. The air feels heavy, pregnant with unspoken words.

'I guess I'd better go home now.' I move to open the door.

'Wait.'

Rob shifts round in his seat. He leans towards me and pauses to check I'm not recoiling, then kisses me gently on my right cheek.

I stop breathing.

'Was that okay?'

I let my breath out audibly.

'Yes . . . Yes. Thanks. Yes.'

* * *

We exchange text messages on Saturday and arrange to meet for coffee before church the following evening. Something tells me I'm going to become a regular attender again.

At the café, we start to share a little more about our lives. He baulks a little when I tell him how much time I've spent in hospital.

'You mean two weeks?'

'No, it really is a total of two years. At least.'

He sits back in his armchair and shakes his head.

'Wow. I'm just so glad you're doing better now.'

'Me too.'

But the conversation moves on, and we lose ourselves in the moment so much that we're almost late for the service.

We sit close together in a pew halfway up the left-hand side, close to Esther and her family who are in their usual seats in the middle. She casts me a slightly nervous look. I flash a smile back at her. I know there are other eyes on us too. My fingers and toes tingle and electric shocks run through my spine.

Afterwards, we talk with the group of guys whom Rob usually hangs around with. His face is bright as he introduces me to each of them. I stand tall and lift my chin as I toss my hair back.

Esther sidles up to me and I give her a hug.

'Esther, this is my friend Rob – he goes to my writing class. Rob, this is Esther.'

'Nice to meet you, Rob.'

'Nice to meet you too.'

Esther has to go, but tells me she'll be in touch about a cuppa during the week. I thank her and say goodbye with what I know is an inane grin on my face.

The guys disperse and Rob asks me if I want to go for a drive. I do. We end up stopping beside another coffee shop, but we sit in the car for a few minutes. He strokes my right hand. 'Are we . . . ?'

'More than friends?'

'Ye-es. Are we?'

'I think so.'

'I think so too.'

'So I can call you my boyfriend?'

'Yes. You can call me your boyfriend . . . which I guess makes you my girlfriend.'

I giggle, and he does too.

'Well, girlfriend, would you like to get some hot chocolate?'

'Yes, boyfriend, I would indeed.'

* * *

The next few weeks are a bit of a whirlwind. Rob and I go to two more concerts and two more films, and we spend all of our Wednesday afternoons after class together – sometimes having lunch, coffee and dinner in succession. Esther observes that we have spent more time in each other's company in six weeks than she and Frank did in their first six months!

We start phoning each other every morning and every evening. Both of us have a deal on our landlines whereby the first fifty-nine minutes are free. Sometimes we have to hang up at fifty-nine minutes and redial – twice! My usual routine melts away as I start to build my life around this new relationship.

At the end of February, we go out to a fancy restaurant to celebrate Rob's birthday. I give him a card which says, 'To my soulmate.' He chokes a little on his soup. Then he smiles, reads the card again and squeezes my hand. I'm a bit audacious. But it's okay.

Eager to see Rob, I become a regular at church again, which pleases Esther and Lesley. And I still have my daily worship sessions with playlists I have chosen to encourage and motivate me. It feels easy to love God when things are going so well. I share a verse with my friends online:

Not only so, but we also glory in our sufferings, because we
know that suffering produces perseverance; perseverance,
character; and character, hope.
(Romans 5:3–4)

I feel that, at last, the sufferings I have endured are leading to
something. My perseverance has somehow developed my character,
and with this new relationship has come hope.

For a few months, Rob and I seem to develop a deeper understanding of each other. We meet each other's families, spend time
in each other's homes, go for lots of long and bracing walks and
enjoy Belfast's buzzing arts scene. We also keep writing, often
sharing projects we don't have confidence to bring to the whole
class. It feels intimate. It feels exciting.

And I am not ill. I am taking quite a cocktail of tablets, some
treating side effects of drugs that treat the side effects of other drugs.
It's like a medicinal game of dominoes. But I don't question it for a
second. I don't want to need hospital ever again.

I have a new psychiatrist, Dr Birch, because I have been referred
to a psychosis service, and I don't like her very much. In three
appointments, she has seen me for a total of nine minutes – I timed
her. It is always a case of 'You're doing okay – I'm not going to
change anything', which in some ways is reasonable. But she doesn't
seem to want to get to know me.

Still, when I tell her that I have a boyfriend, she frowns and looks
down her nose at me.

'I don't think you should be in a relationship. You're not well.
Somebody is going to get hurt.'

Her stare is piercing. I look at my clasped hands. Surely there is
potential for hurt in any relationship. I resolve to ignore her. But her
words echo in my brain. I shouldn't be in a relationship . . . shouldn't
be in a relationship . . . shouldn't . . . shouldn't . . . shouldn't.

I tell Rob for the sake of transparency, but assure him that Dr
Birch doesn't even know me. He crinkles his nose and wipes his
brow.

'Why would your psychiatrist say that?'

'I don't know. But you know me, don't you? Do you not think our relationship is healthy?'

'Ye-es.'

I can tell he's a little unnerved. I tell him that everything is going to be okay. But is it?

14

This doesn't feel like 'friends'
Wrestling with risk

I'm sitting at the dining table in my apartment with my laptop in front of me, doodling with my pen on a notepad as I think about my next sentence. It's Monday evening and I haven't finished my writing class homework for Wednesday, but it's flowing pretty well now and I'm looking forward to sharing it.

At around 9 pm, I close my curtains and switch to artificial light. The room swirls for a second. Vertigo? I sit down and feel a bit better, but I've lost track of what I'm writing and I lean back for a second or two, dragging my fingers through my hair.

It's difficult to regain my focus, so I doodle some more. My thoughts are dispersing to the four corners of the room. They leave an empty space. Maybe it's time to make a cup of tea.

But before I can get up, a thought comes in to fill the gap.

'You are going to kill Rob with a knife.'

I put my hand to my head. What? That's not my thought. Where did that come from?

There it is again, as clear as if it was audible.

'You are going to stab Rob to death.'

The room is swirling again, and I have frozen in my chair.

I feel cold sweat running down my chest. This can't be happening.

I need help, but I can hardly call my boyfriend.

I reach for my phone and dial Olivia's mobile instead. I don't really expect her to pick up, but she does.

'Sharon?'

'Yes. I know it's not the usual time, but . . .'

'I'm taking a lunch break. Are you okay?'

'No. No, I'm really not okay.'

'What's the matter? You haven't taken something?'

'No, no. It's not that. I've been having thoughts. Bad thoughts. Seriously bad.'

'What kind of thoughts?'

'Olivia, I think I'm going to kill Rob.'

'Whatever do you mean?'

'I keep having this thought. It's like it came from nowhere. I felt weird, then my mind was kind of empty – and this thought came in. I am meant to kill Rob with a knife.'

Olivia's volume goes up a few decibels.

'You are what? Have you told Rob this?'

'Oh, no. No way. He already phoned earlier. He's out with friends tonight.'

'Sharon, you can't tell him. Wait . . . Actually, I think you have to tell him.'

'I have to tell him?'

'Sharon, I don't think you're going to act on this thought – really I don't. But you can't tell me that you're going to kill someone and expect me not to inform them. But if you do it, I won't have to.'

'But if you don't think I'm going to act . . .'

'Do you think you're going to act on it?'

'I couldn't – I couldn't hurt Rob. I love him. I love him so much. He's all I care about.'

'I know, and I think that's just the thing. It makes sense that your brain malfunctions in the area that is generating the most thoughts. You are thinking about him all the time. Obsessive thoughts sabotage what's good.'

I feel dizzy again.

'What?'

'I know. It sounds crazy. But I genuinely think this thought has just come from a glitch in your brain. If you didn't care for Rob, I don't think you'd ever have had this thought.'

I'm crying now.

'Uh . . . But do I have to tell him then?'

'Absolutely. There's a theoretical risk. And anyhow, you talk to him so much! He knows you. He'll know something's wrong. You're sick again. He has to know that.'

'I'm actually seeing Dr Birch tomorrow. Can I wait to see what her opinion is?'

'I'm sure she'll agree with me, but I guess that would be okay.'

I grasp my forehead with one hand and push the phone closer in to my ear with the other.

'O-o-oh!'

'What is it?'

'It's playing over and over again in my brain.'

Olivia's voice is calm.

'Think. What can you do to stop it? Use your distraction techniques.'

'It won't stop until I do it.'

'But you're not planning to do it, right?'

'I couldn't do it. I'd kill myself first.'

Olivia sighs.

'That would be my worry, really. Can you keep yourself safe until you get to Dr Birch?'

'Okay.'

'What does okay mean?'

Tears are streaming down my face. My words are punctuated by sobs.

'I'll keep . . . myself . . . safe.'

'You'll get through this.'

'No relationship . . . can survive . . . this . . .'

'We'll see. Stay hopeful. Listen, I have to go, but call me if you need me and I'll get a moment to get back to you somehow. Go to bed and get some sleep.'

Ha. Sleep? I feel like I'll never rest easy again.

'Thanks.'

I sob.

'Bye.'

'Bye.'

I get up from my chair and shut down my laptop. My eyes are burning and my stomach hurts.

Why? Why? This stupid, stupid illness. I hate it.

* * *

The following morning, Rob doesn't call me. He's been out late, and I'm not going to take the initiative. I'll call him once I've seen Dr Birch.

I don't have to wait long for my ten o'clock appointment. Dr Birch never uses a full ten-minute slot with her patients, so she's always bang on time.

'Sharon!'

Her intonation indicates a command, not an invitation, to follow her. I do, and she offers me a chair in her tiny but organized consulting room.

'Well, tell me how you're doing. Did changing to the liquid antipsychotic help your reflux any?'

I am not interested in reflux, but I nod anyway.

She detects a change in my demeanour.

'Is something wrong?'

I tug my skirt down towards my knees.

'I'm not doing well.'

'What's happened?'

'I'm having these thoughts –'

'What kind of thoughts?' Dr Birch rarely allows me to finish a sentence.

I take a deep breath and spit it out.

'I had thoughts of killing Rob – my boyfriend.'

'What?!'

She's sitting up in her swivel chair now, eyebrows raised, pen poised as if it were she who might stab somebody.

I claw back.

'They're just thoughts. They're not my thoughts. I don't recognize them. I don't want to hurt him. I couldn't. I don't want to hurt anyone. Honestly, I couldn't.'

'You're telling me that you have had thoughts of killing your boyfriend?'

'Yes, but –'

'Have you told him about this?'

'Not yet.'

'Well, I'm going to have to tell him. You know there are limits to confidentiality.'

'I'm not going to act on the thoughts. Honestly.'

'We can't be sure of that. It sounds like you've been having command hallucinations. People do act on this kind of thought.'

I bite my cheek hard and loosen my cardigan.

'I'll tell him then.'

'You promise me that it will be the first thing you do when you leave here?'

I nod, wiping a tissue across my face.

'Yes.'

'I think I will make a referral to our forensic psychiatrist.'

My eyes widen.

'But I haven't done anything.'

'I know, but you need to be assessed. What you've told me today must be taken very seriously.'

I'm sobbing again. Not only is my relationship about to be over, but I'm being treated as a potential murderer.

It's the first time we've passed the ten-minute mark in a consultation.

'I'm not going to detain you right now, but I may need to. What is your boyfriend – Bob, is it? – what is his phone number?'

'It's Rob.'

I call out his phone number.

Dr Birch seems to have gathered herself, but she is still pointing her pen at me.

'Right, this has to be sorted today. I'm going to call you at around 4 pm, and if you haven't told Bob by then, I'll ring him. I'm going to call your GP too.'

'I'll call Rob as soon as I get home.'

'Good.'

She's taken this so seriously. Maybe I am a risk to Rob. This will be the end of something so good. Shouldn't be in a relationship . . . shouldn't . . . shouldn't . . . Was she right after all?

* * *

Back at home, I pause. The thoughts aren't there any more, but I'm scared they'll come back.

I put my scrunched-up tissues in the bin and splash cold water on my face.

Shaking, I pull up Rob's number on my phone. I stifle a cry of pain as I touch the screen.

He answers quickly and brightly.

'Hello.'

'Hi.'

'Ah, it's wee Shazzie. I missed you this morning, but I'm in town. Shall I come over?'

'Rob, I have to tell you something . . .'

I'm fighting back tears. My voice is raspy.

'Are you okay?'

'No. No, I'm not. Sorry. I'm so sorry.'

His tone changes.

'What for, love?'

'I was with my psychiatrist . . .'

'Oh yes, I forgot to ask you about that. Did it not go well?'

'I've had these thoughts. I have to tell you.'

His tone is kind, gentle.

'What sort of thoughts?'

'I would never, ever act on them. I couldn't. I love you.'

Rob clears his throat.

'What are you talking about?'

'I – I had thoughts that I was going to kill you. I told her I wouldn't act on them. They're not my thoughts. I don't know where they're coming from. It was just last night. I'm sorry. I'm so sorry.'

Rob's voice is squeaky.

'You thought about . . . Uh . . . So I shouldn't come over?'

135

'No. I mean – I don't know. It's up to you. I know I won't do it. Really, truly.'

'It's your illness, isn't it? But what did Dr Birch think?'

'She told me I had to tell you, or she would tell you.'

'So she thought I might be in danger?'

My phone slides through my hand but I catch it before it hits the ground.

'I won't do it . . . Honestly . . . You're all I care about . . .'

My sobbing is barely controllable.

He doesn't reply immediately. I ask him if he's okay.

'Mm, it's heavy stuff.'

'I know.'

'I mean, it's a new situation for me, obviously. No one expects that their girlfriend is going to think about killing them.'

'I know. I'm so sorry.'

'So, are we meant to break up?'

'Do you want that?'

I can picture Rob, his eyes gazing into the distance, lips pursed.

'Shazzie, I don't know what to do. I'm just – just a bit shocked, I suppose. Were you not going to tell me if Dr Birch hadn't told you to?'

'I would have. Honestly.'

Maybe.

There's silence. I've run out of tissues, but I don't care.

Rob speaks first.

'I don't know how to deal with this.'

'Do you want to break up?'

'It's not that I want to. But, I mean, how were you going to kill me?'

I whimper.

'With a knife.'

He fails to disguise a gasp.

'Uh . . . Right.'

'I understand if you want to end it.'

'I guess that's what the psychiatrist wanted all along, wasn't it?'

'Yes, but –'

Rob is breathing heavily.

'Sharon, maybe it's best if we go along with what she says. She's an expert. I'm not.'

'So that's it, then?'

I can hardly get the words out.

'I guess so.'

He sighs.

'I'll miss you so much, Robbie.'

'It's not what we would have wanted.'

'No.'

'Well. Goodbye, then.'

'Goodbye.'

The phone clicks off. I slide on to the wooden floor. It's over. My relationship. My life. And it's all my fault.

* * *

I stumble my way round the corner to my GP surgery. I've made an urgent appointment with Dr Oates.

A couple of lines from a local songwriter, Ruth Trimble, whom Rob and I both love, turn over and over in my head.

> I'll take your number off the wall,
> try to remember not to call,
> and when I finally find a way to let you go . . .[1]

Let you go? I sniff. I'll never, never be able to let Rob go. I will never love anyone else. How could I anyway? I'd have to give a caveat: 'I broke up with my ex because I had thoughts of killing him.' I am finished.

I trip on a broken paving stone. Tears are streaming down my face and passers-by look at me, but I don't care. Nothing matters any more.

I finger my phone in my pocket. 'Try to remember not to call.' Rob is the only person I want to talk to, but he's off limits now. I'll talk to Dr Oates instead. She'll know what to do . . . Won't she?

In the waiting room, I try to count the ceiling tiles. It's a 'grounding exercise' I've learnt from the psychologist. Take note of your surroundings – sights, sounds, smells. It doesn't work. All I can see is Rob's kind face. All I can hear is his distinctive bass voice. All I can smell is his aftershave.

I bite my lower lip so hard that it bleeds.

Eventually, the bell dings and my name appears on the LED screen above my head.

I shuffle my way to Dr Oates's room and knock on the door.

'Come on in.'

I enter and sit down, pulling yet another packet of tissues from my bag.

Dr Oates has long, brown hair. It swishes as she swivels in her chair and she rolls into the middle of the room. She pats my leg and I look into her broad face. Her eyes fix mine and she shakes her head.

'You know?'

'Yes. Dr Birch called me at lunchtime, so I thought I might see you this afternoon. I'm glad you're here.'

'Dr Oates, it's over. I never should have been in a relationship. Dr Birch said somebody would get hurt and now everyone has got hurt. Rob won't cope with this. I can't cope – I want to die.'

'Sharon.' Her tone is firm. 'I don't think this needs to be the end.'

I blow my nose and look up.

'What do you mean? I'm a risk to him.'

'I don't think Dr Birch knows you as well as I do. Would you agree?'

My cheeks are hot. I unzip my jacket.

'She's never spent any time with me. One day I got a taxi to see her and the driver hadn't pulled away by the time the appointment was finished.'

'Exactly. Whereas you've probably spent twenty minutes a week with me for the past three years . . .'

I stop crying for a second.

'Sharon, Dr Birch thinks you're having command hallucinations. Those are dangerous.'

Her face is deadly serious. She goes on.

'But I think you are having obsessive thoughts, which are part of obsessive-compulsive disorder (OCD – remember, they said you had that in America?) and are not dangerous.'

I sit a little straighter.

'That's what Olivia, my aunt, said. That the thought came because I was thinking about Rob so much.'

'Exactly. A person who doesn't have OCD gets a strange thought and they can just dismiss it; a person with OCD gets a strange thought and fixates on it.'

'But thoughts about killing someone . . .'

Dr Oates lifts her chin.

'Not uncommon.'

A ray of sunlight suddenly penetrates the window. My heart starts racing.

'So I'm not a danger to Rob?'

'I haven't convinced Dr Birch of that yet, but I'm confident you're not. Probably even less of a danger now that you have got so upset by your thoughts. You'd probably do anything to avoid acting on them.'

'I'd kill myself first.'

'I believe you.'

'But I've told Rob and now he's scared and we've broken up and everything is a mess.'

Dr Oates grimaces.

'I know. It's not easy.'

'Is Dr Birch still going to refer me to the forensic psychiatrist?'

'I don't think so.'

I've stopped crying.

'What should I do?'

The doctor leans back in her chair and puts a finger to her cheek.

'Maybe try to meet with Rob – somewhere neutral – public – where he won't feel as if he's in danger, and explain what I've said.'

'Right.'

'And I think we'll maybe try to find you a better psychiatrist. One who will take time with you.'

I nod.

'Let me know how it goes.'

'I will.'

* * *

Freda, our church's pastoral care worker, has a blue living room with long windows hung with drapes in muted colours. Danny, the pastor, is sitting in an armchair by the fireplace. I am on the edge of a sofa next to the door, hunched, twiddling my thumbs one way and then the other. Even in the June light, the air seems thick and grey.

'I'm sure he'll be here soon.'

Danny opens his hands wide and claps them together.

Freda offers me a cup of tea. I accept, but my throat is too tight to swallow.

We hear the crunch of tyres on gravel. Danny looks at me and flashes his most earnest and encouraging smile. Freda jumps up.

'I'll just get the door.'

When Rob comes in, murmuring apologies – heavy traffic coming into Belfast – his shirt is a bit crumpled and his eyes are red, though not as red as mine. Danny indicates that he should take the chair opposite him, and he eases himself into it stiffly.

'Tea or coffee, Rob?'

'Ah, I'll take a coffee please, Freda.'

She pours a mug for him, but he doesn't touch it.

'Ahem.' Danny points one open hand towards me and one towards Rob. 'We all know why we're here, I hope. I realize that something very sad has played out this week – for both of you, Sharon and Rob.'

I try to curl my lips into a smile. Rob exhales noisily.

'I know that there was a very sudden ending to what had been a hopeful – and quite intense – relationship, and the circumstances have not been exactly . . . usual, shall we say?'

I swallow, hard. Rob nods.

'Sharon, do you want to tell us how you're feeling?'

I do. I want to tell everyone that it's all just been a big mistake and it was just a thought and I shouldn't have let it be blown out of proportion. That I just wanted – above everything – for Rob to be safe. And that I don't know how I am going to go on without him, that he completed me, that I truly love him in a way that I have never felt before.

But I say nothing. I can't contain my sobbing. Freda gets me some more tissues.

'We know it's very hard for you, Sharon. Rob, do you have anything to say?'

Rob chokes. His face is red and he's grasping his knees with his hands.

'Sharon is a very . . . special . . . girl . . . I don't understand what's happening . . . I've never been in this situation before.'

Danny nods. 'It is a very peculiar situation. I just want to acknowledge that. And I imagine that you have been quite frightened.'

Rob hesitates, then nods.

'But – but I never really thought Sharon wanted to hurt me. I know it's her illness. I know she's not well. I just don't know what this means for us – for me. I mean, do we have to stop going to the same church? Same writing classes?'

Freda leans in.

'I don't think so, Rob. You weren't here when Sharon was explaining it, but her GP really thinks the thoughts she is having are obsessions – unwanted thoughts that are hard to get rid of, but which people almost never act on.'

Rob raises one eyebrow.

'Obsessions? The psychiatrist said they were some kind of hallucinations.'

Freda is a qualified doctor too.

'I know. And that's possible, but Sharon's psychiatrist doesn't know her as well as her GP. I know Sharon well too, and I think her GP might be right.'

I wrap my cardigan around me tight and try to speak. I hear myself groan instead.

'Would you like to say something, Sharon?'

Danny's tone is coaxing.

I turn to Rob, my teary eyes beseeching him to listen.

'I'm sure that's what they are – obsessions. Honey – sorry, I mean Rob – I thought about you so much it's like my mind was eventually going to make a mistake. If I was like a normal person, I would just have dismissed it as nonsense, but my brain is not – normal. You know that . . .'

Danny has noticed that Rob is crying.

'Are you okay, Rob?'

'Yes. No. I mean, it's a bit surreal.'

'It seems like you are both very sad about the end of something that you had which was good. You have decisions ahead of you. I think you both need time to process what has happened. Sharon, you have your doctors to talk to, or Freda, or Esther. Rob, you probably don't feel like you can talk about this to anyone. But you can always call me. I want to be here for you.'

Danny pauses for a second.

'And we know that there's Someone even greater than any problem human minds can dream up – Someone we can talk to at any hour of the day or night. Because we have a God who understands us fully. Psalm 139 verse 16 tells us that before any of our days came to be, they were written in his book. He knows what the future looks like for both of you.'

Freda puts a hand on my shoulder. Rob blows his nose.

Danny sits forward in his chair.

'Can I pray for you guys?'

'Yes.'

'Yes.'

'Father God. We bring your children, Sharon and Rob, before you now. They both love you and we know that you surround them with compassion. How they need to feel your presence today, Lord. We pray for Sharon, whose battles with illness you know intimately, that she would feel your healing touch and know the hope that only you can bring. We pray for Rob, that you would heal him too from the pain and hurt that he feels right now. Please give both of them wisdom, give the doctors wisdom, give us as pastoral carers wisdom.

Help all of us to know the best way forward. And regardless of whatever decisions Sharon and Rob may take about their lives in the next days and weeks, help them to keep focused on you, so that everything else can fall into its proper place. Go with us as we leave this place today. We thank you for your presence with us. Amen.'

As we all straighten up from our hunched prayer positions, I cast a quick glance at Rob. He smiles at me, but with sad eyes.

Danny stands up.

'How are you getting home, Sharon?'

'Oh, I'll just walk.'

Rob gets out his car keys.

'I can take her . . . if you'd like that, Sharon?'

I look at Danny for approval. He shrugs.

'Ye-es. Thanks, uh, Rob.'

We drive the few minutes to my apartment building in silence, but when we park, Rob lets out a sob.

'Are you okay?'

'Oh, Sharon, it's just – just that you looked so forlorn in there. I never wanted to see you like that.'

'I'm sorry.'

He takes a swig from a bottle of sugar-free cola in his drink holder, and his tears dry.

'Thanks for the lift.'

'That's okay.'

I swing my legs out of the car.

'Sharon, wait!'

'What is it?'

'Uh. Do you want to come down on Saturday – as a friend, just – and go to the gym with me?'

My heart skips a beat.

'You won't be scared?'

'I'll hide the knives.'

I don't know if he's joking or serious. I find myself smiling anyway.

'Okay. I'll come.'

'Alright, love – I mean Sharon. I'll see you then.'
Friends. It's something.

* * *

I arrive at Rob's at 11 am on Saturday, wearing a nice hoodie and a pair of jeans, and with my kit bag over my shoulder.

'Let's have a cuppa before we go, shall we?'

Rob puts the kettle on. We stand against the kitchen counters at opposite sides of the room, arms folded.

'Here, do you want a hug – friend to friend?'

I do. More than anything. I walk over to him slowly and allow him to enfold me in his arms. I am ready to pull back, but he draws me closer. I can smell his familiar smell, feel his breath on my neck. I snuggle my head into his shoulder and he kisses my crown.

'Robbie?'

'Shazzie?'

'This doesn't feel a lot like "friends", does it?'

'I guess it doesn't.'

15

It's not your average relationship
Wrestling with first love

All the knives have been locked away and Rob and I are 'more than friends' again, but the ride is bumpy.

First, Rob gets sick. We are away for a few days at a residential literary summer school, having both won writing scholarships to attend. On the penultimate night, Rob tells me he feels more tired than usual. The next morning, when I meet him in the foyer before the first session, he looks grey and sweat is dripping from his brow.

'Are you okay?'

I take his hand. It feels dry and hot.

'I don't know. There's a funny feeling in my chest.'

'Honey, we're going to have to get you home. You're burning up.'

'I'll be okay – it's the last day. I'll make it through.'

He wipes his brow, but his handkerchief is too wet to absorb much more.

'Come on, you can't sit in a theatre like this.'

'Could you get me a drink of water?'

I approach the bar, not yet open, and ask a girl who is sweeping the floor for a glass. She pours the water and asks me if I want ice in it. I do. The cooler I can get Rob, the better.

Rob takes a few sips.

'You're dehydrated. You need to take as much of that as possible.'

'It's just that I feel a bit nauseous.'

I look him up and down. He's probably going to need a doctor.

'Listen, you need to drive home before you get too sick to make the journey.'

'I wanted to hear Mike Laney at lunchtime.'

'I know, but sickness comes to inconvenience us at times. Believe me – I know all about it.'

He smiles, then coughs.

'Okay then.'

We drive back to his house and call the doctor for advice. A GP is able to see him late in the afternoon and quickly diagnoses a nasty chest infection. She prescribes some antibiotics, paracetamol or ibuprofen to take the fever down, and plenty of rest and clear fluids.

I know that Rob is likely to take to his bed and neglect all of the above.

'I'm going to stay with you. In the guest room. I'll make you meals and keep the housework ticking over. Just for a few days until you're feeling stronger again.'

Rob sighs. He squeezes my hand.

'Okay then. Thanks.'

It turns out to be more than a few days. For three weeks I never stray far from Rob's bed. I make cold compress after cold compress for his head, coax him to drink, change his sheets after the fevers, make thin soups and keep track of doses of anti-inflammatories and painkillers.

Two more courses of antibiotics later, Rob is sitting up in his chair, still coughing, but with a pinkish tinge to his cheeks where there had been only grey before.

It is time for me to move out again, but I leave changed. Deep in my heart, after six complicated months of dating, I know that I want to be the one who looks after this man until death do us part. I tell him so, and he laughs. But something has changed in him too.

'Don't take this the wrong way, but I never really thought you could be this steady – this capable. I don't honestly know if I'd have made it through without you. You're right that I probably wouldn't have eaten or drunk enough – maybe I'd have ended up in hospital. Thanks, Shazzie. I'm going to tell everyone how amazing you are.'

Driving home, I smile the whole way. I have been able to show love to Rob in a very tangible way, and I'm certain now that he loves me too.

But just because we've both seen each other through hard times doesn't mean that things are going to be easy or straightforward from now on. We have a few more obstacles ahead.

The first is mania.

When Rob calls me one Friday afternoon, I am dancing with my mop around my living room. I've been cleaning all day and I am just so excited about my plans to redecorate my flat in pink and purple.

'What are you doing?'

I giggle.

'Do you still want to meet for dinner before the play tonight?'

I laugh so hard that it ends in an unattractive snort.

'I didn't realize I was so funny . . .'

'Oh, it's not you – it's the polka dots and the dancing heffalumps.'

I laugh again and my chest wheezes, so that I sound like a broken accordion.

'Sharon, are you not well?'

'Well? Not well? Well, well, well. Of course I'm well!'

I start singing.

'Listen, I think you need to take some diazepam. I'm going to come over as soon as I can. You won't go out anywhere, will you? Please stay put until I can help you.'

'Are you bringing some paint?'

'Paint?'

'For my project!'

'I think we'll leave painting for another day, shall we?'

It takes Rob an hour to get organized and another hour to drive up to the city. By the time he arrives in the car park, all my windows are open and 'Dancing queen' is blasting from my speakers. I spot him pulling up and run out to greet him, skipping and shouting.

'SShhh! Stop that, Shazzie. What are you doing in there? What will the neighbours think? Come on, let's get that thing turned down.'

Rob ushers me back inside and quickly closes all the windows. I run from room to room, jumping up to touch the ceilings and singing along to my *Abba Gold*.

'I'm going to have to ring Dr Oates. I can't take you out like this.'

'But I'm so happy! I'm so excited about the play. Play, yay, yay, hey!'

'You're not – yourself. I've never seen you like this. Here, sit down!'

Dr Oates is not on duty. Her colleague, Dr Parks, tells Rob that it sounds like mania is setting in again, and since it's 5.30 on a Friday evening, the best option is to take me to A&E. They'll know what to do.

Rob loosens his tie. There go the theatre tickets. He sighs. Those weren't cheap.

The Accident and Emergency Department is crowded already and likely to become more so as Belfast's Friday night revellers begin to collapse or punch each other.

I find it all very exciting.

'I feel just like a doctor – isn't that just wonderful?'

'Sit down beside me and try to keep quiet. People are sick.'

'But Robbie, I don't need to be here.'

'Believe me, you need help – we need help.'

I pace up and down the department, narrowly avoiding a collision with a mobile X-ray unit and upsetting nurses by looking over their shoulders as they make notes.

I delight in making my own diagnoses. A man is vomiting behind a curtain. Someone wheels in a unit of blood on a drip stand. Oesophageal varices? A plaintive child has her arm in a makeshift sling. Greenstick fracture. A pregnant lady caresses her bump. Probably hasn't felt her baby move in a day or two.

I pass Rob as I continue my 'ward round'.

'Sharon, sit here!'

I sit down and plant a great big kiss on his cheek. He wipes my lipstick off.

'Stop that!'

I get up again and continue my pacing. I overhear Rob asking a nurse when I am likely to be seen. She reassures him that it will be as soon as possible, and the 'Mental Health at Night Team' have been told that I am here as well.

A man with a sheet-white face who is holding his chest is rushed past me to the resuscitation bay. Heart attack? I try to follow, but this time Sister asks me in a very firm tone to sit down. I obey, but I can't rest for long.

'Sharon, I can't cope with this.'

'What do you mean?'

Rob's hands are on his ears.

'This place is chaos. It's too noisy, and you won't sit with me anyway. I'm going to the play.'

'Without me?'

'Sharon, you can't possibly go in this state. I'll come back afterwards. It could be hours before you're seen.'

Rob leaves. I am surprised, but I'm too activated to be unduly distressed. I pace and pace and watch all that is going on around me. Two hours pass easily enough. He comes back just as a young man with a clipboard and a longish beard calls me into a side room.

'I'm the psychiatry registrar. Are you with Sharon?'

'Yes, I'm her boyfriend.'

'Then maybe you can help with the history.'

For the whole duration of the interview, I walk in circles around the room, occasionally getting dizzy enough to fall on to a chair or into Rob's lap before pushing myself back up again.

'Right.' The doctor slaps his clipboard down on his knees. 'We know that you have a mood disorder, Sharon, and it's obvious that you're in an elevated state. But I don't think you're a danger to yourself, as long as you're not left alone. I'm going to ask the Home Treatment Team to visit you tomorrow morning. In the meantime, I want to give you an increased dose of your antipsychotic and some extra diazepam. You might be able to get a couple of hours' sleep.'

Rob drives me home.

'I hope we never, ever have to go to A&E again. That was awful.'

The medication helps to settle me, and the Home Treatment Team doctors are able to make some more enduring changes over the weekend. It takes a couple of weeks, but I regain my equilibrium.

'I can't quite believe you left me to go to the theatre!'

'Sharon, you hardly noticed. It was absolutely the right thing to do at the time.'

We can laugh about it in retrospect, but neither of us wants me to get manic ever again.

And then there are the depressive episodes.

'Sharon, you've been on this sofa for two weeks. How long is this going to last?'

'I don't know – a few more weeks? Sometimes it's months.'

'We can't go months without a date. Am I going to have to sell those concert tickets for next Friday again?'

'I'm sorry. It's not me; it's the depression.'

Rob is sitting on a chair at the end of my living room. He gets up and pours himself a glass of juice from the fridge, then squeezes on to the sofa beside me.

'Here, let's just go for a little walk in the park. The kids won't be out of school yet – you'll not meet many people.'

I curl up even more tightly, hugging my knees. Rob strokes my cheek.

'Come on. You can do it. I'll take your arm.'

I turn my face into a cushion.

'Please.'

I sneak a look at his face and loosen a little.

'Okay. Just a short walk. Short, okay?'

Rob jumps up. He wants to go before I change my mind.

It's a bright autumn day, and Rob takes a few photos of the changing foliage, but to me it feels like dusk. The air is still, yet I see the shadows of the trees moving, swirling. The birdsong sounds too shrill. I feel suspicious of the man exercising his dog in the open space to the right of the path.

I cling to Rob's arm more and more tightly.

'What's wrong, pet?'

'I have to get home.'

'It's not much further. Look at all those colours – it's beautiful!'

'No. No, seriously – we need to turn back.'

I can feel it now, tracking us.

'Okay, then. Just let me get a pic of this oak.'

'No, please. Please, let's go!'

'What's wrong? You look like you've seen a ghost.'

'The evil presence is following me. It's over my left shoulder again.'

'The evil presence? I don't see anything.'

'I know. You can't. It's in the fourth dimension. Please, get me home.'

'You're psychotic, Sharon.'

'You shouldn't have brought me here.'

Rob shrugs.

'Sorry.'

We turn back. I shudder every few steps and whimper quietly to myself. After what seems like a lifetime, we arrive back at the apartment.

'Should I call the doctor for you?'

I'm crying now. I cast a furtive glance into the corners where the ceiling meets the walls.

'What are you seeing?'

I choke.

'Right, you gave me your GP's number. I'm going to use it.'

I take a swig from the juice Rob has left on the coffee table.

The on-call doctor tells Rob to bring me round to see him at the end of his afternoon surgery. It's Dr Parks again – not my regular GP, but someone who knows me reasonably well.

'You've had this – this "presence" – before, haven't you, Sharon?'

I nod.

'And I think a small increase in your antipsychotic helped, didn't it?'

'I think so.'

'Well, let's do that again.'

Rob clears his throat.

'She's been really depressed as well. Haven't you, Sharon?'

I nod again.

'Hmm. That's a bit harder for me to address right now. It's not long since you were a bit manic, sure it's not? We don't want to give you anything that would trigger that again. Sharon, do you think you can lie low until you see your psychiatrist again?'

I have a new psychiatrist – one who specializes in treating sick doctors. I trust him.

'Ye-es.'

As we drive back to my apartment, Rob sighs.

'What's wrong?'

'It's just that, you know, this is really hard. I mean, it's not like your average relationship, is it?'

I stiffen.

'You've had enough of me?'

'No. No, it's not like that. I think so highly of you. I love being with you. But we can't plan anything ahead, and you are just so sick so often.'

We have a lot of conversations like this over the next couple of years. It is hard for Rob. He wants to go places, make memories together. It's hard for me too. When I'm sick, I feel under pressure to be well for him.

But there are a lot of good times too, in between the 'episodes'.

We have brunch after church every Sunday and then walk miles along the coast, often ending with a visit to my granny in her seaside nursing home.

We meet at the cinema every Monday night and discuss the film afterwards in McDonald's, often staying until closing time.

We go to Rob's gym on Saturdays and relax afterwards in the pool and sauna.

We have one dinner a week in his house and one at my apartment, and when the occasion calls for something a bit more special, we take turns to pick favourite restaurants.

We go to a Bible study in a country mission hall on Tuesday evenings, learning together from God's word and spending time with friends.

And there are stand-out one-off moments too – visiting the London Eye and going to Wimbledon to watch the tennis; climbing Slieve Donard, the highest peak in Northern Ireland; Rob's first flying lesson (with me an excited passenger); visiting the Writers Museum in Dublin; walking among the cows on the strand at White Park Bay and dancing in the waves; spending two wonderful weeks in California with Aunt Olivia and Uncle Peter . . . The list goes on.

With my nagging encouragement, Rob begins a master's degree in creative writing. He graduates after a year of steep learning curves and long, long nights in front of his laptop, and the screenplay he produces for his dissertation project is read by several Hollywood film producers.

Meanwhile, after a few months of relative stability, I get a part-time paid job in another constituency office. I love the work and the routine it brings with it. I grow in confidence as I meet members of the public and deal with officials at the council and the Stormont Assembly. And the extra income means that I can book some more evenings out to enjoy with my beloved.

With Rob at my side, I am a regular attender at church again, and faith starts to play more and more of a role in how I manage my illness.

Certain Scripture verses become particularly important to me.

There's Paul in Philippians 4:8: 'Finally, brothers and sisters, whatever is true, whatever is noble, whatever is right, whatever is pure, whatever is lovely, whatever is admirable – if anything is excellent or praiseworthy – think about such things.' When tormentors and presences flood my mind, I turn to this verse and try to replace them with lovely thoughts. I print out a few favourite photographs to remind me of what is good in my life; I buy a bunch of flowers to brighten my room; I listen to worship music. It all helps.

Then there are Jesus' words in John 16:33: 'In this world you will have trouble. But take heart! I have overcome the world.' They remind me that no one – least of all Jesus – said that the Christian life would be easy, with or without mental illness, but that the battle is already won.

Psalm 139, which Danny quoted, becomes very dear to me too. When my world feels black, I am reminded that 'even the darkness will not be dark to [God]; the night will shine like the day, for darkness is as light to [him]' (verse 12). I remember that God 'created my inmost being' (verse 13) and that 'all the days ordained for me' were written in God's book (verse 16). God knows me intimately, understands me and holds my future.

And my baptismal blessing, Romans 15:13, takes on new meaning: 'May the God of hope fill you with all joy and peace as you trust in him, so that you may overflow with hope by the power of the Holy Spirit.' If I trust in God, there is always true hope, regardless of whether I am depressed, manic, psychotic or feeling well.

* * *

Pastor Danny meets with Rob and me, as a couple, in the airy upstairs living room of my new flat.

'You two have been together for quite a while now.'

He sips his coffee.

I am quick to reply.

'Over two years.'

Rob shifts his weight on the leatherette sofa.

'Hmm, yes, I thought it must have been around that.'

He looks across to my bookcase. I see him wryly taking note of a copy of *Boundaries in Dating* by Henry Cloud, which sits alone on the top shelf.

'I suppose I've just been wondering whether you have given any thought to the future. I mean, you've had some time to get to know each other. I'm aware there have been difficulties, but here you are, still together. That speaks to me of a strong relationship.'

Rob's colour heightens. I feel the beginnings of a smile, but I stifle it. I've been desperate for someone to initiate this conversation for ages, but I don't want to let it show.

Rob speaks first.

'I think that when one person is living with mental health problems, it puts quite a burden on the relationship. You don't know how things are going to go – whether the person could really cope with . . .'

He tails off and looks out of the window.

'With marriage, you mean?'

Danny's tone is quite sharp.

Rob speaks from behind his hand.

'Marriage is a big commitment.'

'Yes, it is, but it is God's intention for a man and a woman who love each other to enter into the covenant of marriage.'

Rob shifts around again. I take his hand and it's sweaty.

Danny turns to me.

'Sharon, how do you feel about the relationship? Do you love Rob?'

My throat is tight.

'Yes, I really love him. I want to be with him for ever.'

'Do you hear that, Rob? Sharon feels ready for commitment. And I think that's quite normal. Don't you?'

'Ye-es. But it's not an average relationship. We've been through a lot. It's hard to plan for next week, never mind the long term.'

'But Sharon has been well for a while now. She's working; she's involved at church.'

'I know, but there are still hard days. She needs a lot more support than people realize.'

I squirm a little.

Danny clasps his hands together.

'And that's where loving Christian partnership comes into its own. I've seen times when Sharon has been an important support to you too.'

Rob nods slowly.

'Well, I just wanted to start the conversation – out of pastoral concern for you both. The longer a relationship goes on without commitment, the greater the potential for people to get hurt. I want you to think about that, and perhaps we can meet again in a month or two and have another chat. Is that okay?'

'Yes.'

'Of course.'

Danny prays for us. I feel tingles in my fingers. I pray silently too: 'Please, God, please let Rob ask me to marry him.'

I know it is hard for Rob. He has seen me high, he has seen me low, he has seen me tormented and vulnerable. But he has also seen me laughing, wisecracking, contributing intelligently to discussion, holding his hand when he's been grieving or worried about something, making tasty meals for him, doing his ironing, holding him tight in moments of romance.

Danny meets with us fairly regularly over the next few months. We talk about our hopes and our fears. We even have a trial break, but our week apart ends after three days. Neither of us can resist the urge to check that the other is okay.

And some time later, on New Year's Eve, Rob brings out a box. I catch my breath as I realize it has his late mum's rings in it. He picks out the three-stone engagement ring, its gold a little dull but its diamonds still sparkling.

'Would you like to try this one on?'

Laughter bubbles up from within me. I slide it on to my ring finger. It's loose, but it looks stunning. I can barely breathe.

'Does this mean we're engaged?!'

Rob is smiling and holding his hand to his chest.

'Would you like that?'

I don't answer. I rush at him and fling my arms around his neck, crying.

'We're engaged! We're engaged!'

Rob wipes his brow.

'Yes. I guess we are.'

We decide to get married quickly. We're getting older and we've had a three-year courtship already. I am certain that marriage will bring just the stability I need to flourish. I can tell Rob is less convinced, but his love for me has finally overcome his anxieties.

Time will soon tell.

16

Even there your hand will guide
Wrestling, with acceptance

As I sit in the winter sunlight, my engagement ring sparkles. Rob and I have been married for almost four years now. It really has been a journey through severe mental illness for both of us. I have had a dozen hospital admissions, including three during the writing of this book, and I have undergone a series of ECT (electroconvulsive therapy) treatments twice.

* * *

'Why the tears?'

I'm standing in a mirrored elevator with a neat blonde nurse called April who is holding my medical notes.

'I don't know. I guess I just don't want to wake up again after this.'

April raises her eyebrows.

'Well, we'll be doing all we can to make sure you do. Anyway, do you remember how quickly you responded to this in the springtime? Your perspective could be completely changed.'

I shake my head slowly. This time I am hopeless.

The elevator opens and I walk forward robotically. The corridor is cold, and I shiver as we reach the Day Procedure Unit.

The buxom Sister in charge opens the door with a broad smile.

'Ah, Sharon. Come on ahead and we'll get you up on the bed here.'

Dr Tufnell nods in my direction.

'Good morning, Sharon. Still happy to go through with the treatment?'

'Yes.'

What other option do I have?

The anaesthetic nurse, Leanne, puts a blood pressure cuff on my arm and starts to stick leads for a heart monitor on to my chest.

April places a blanket over me and asks if she can slip off my socks. It helps them to keep track of the seizure activity if they can see my toes moving.

There's another mental health nurse working to my right. Geraldine looks at my wristband and calls out my hospital number to April, who checks that it matches up with my notes.

April applies electrodes to my head with an eggy gel. I close my eyes for a second as the room becomes too chaotic, then open them again.

To my left, there is a tall, ginger-haired man with a stethoscope in the pocket of his scrubs.

Leanne introduces him.

'This is Dr Whitley, your anaesthetist for this morning.'

I recognize him instantly. He was in my class at medical school. Consultant anaesthetist, psychiatric patient. How our paths have diverged.

He doesn't recognize me – or doesn't admit to it.

'Good morning, Sharon. I'll be looking after the "sleepy bit" today. Can you just open and close your fist a few times and I'll have this cannula in before you know it.'

The lights above my head are too bright.

'Just a sharp scratch now.'

Dr Whitley has venous access. Dr Tufnell has his machine tuned to his chosen setting. I have leads everywhere and a saline drip running into my left arm. We are ready to go.

April squeezes my hand as Leanne hands me an oxygen mask.

The gas smells of vanilla.

'Take three deep breaths for me.'

Dr Whitley injects propofol and a muscle relaxant into my cannula.

'The anaesthetic is going in now. You might feel a bit warm and tingly.'

I can't wait for the relief of unconsciousness.

One deep breath . . . Two . . .

I'm gone.

* * *

I open my eyes. My head is thumping.

'There you are, love. It's all over.'

Geraldine and April are leaning over me. We're in Recovery. The leads are gone, the cannula has been taken out of my arm and my socks are back on my feet. I feel like I've been away for a very long time.

'We'll get you back to the ward and organize a bite of breakfast for you. I'm sure you're starving.'

'Did it go okay?'

'Yes, love. You had a good seizure. Dr Tufnell was pleased.'

A good seizure. Whatever that is.

As April shoves open the double doors into the ward, the other patients look at me. I'm a curiosity in my wheelchair. Everyone knows that Tuesday is the day for ECT. Electroconvulsive therapy. It sounds terrifying to the uninitiated.

Back in my room, I stretch out on the bed, shielding my eyes from the daylight.

'I'll get your meds now. And Susan is going to bring you some tea and toast.'

'April?'

'Yes?'

'Could you bring me some paracetamol too, please?'

'Of course. You take the liquid, don't you?'

'Please.'

The big round tablets they keep on the ward get stuck in my throat every time.

Susan arrives with my breakfast.

'I brought you two cups of tea. I know you love your tea in the mornings.'

'Thanks so much.'

April pops back in and watches me take my meds. It's nursing policy.

Before she leaves, Glenda, the ward manager, knocks on the door.

'Hi, Sharon. I just wanted to let you know that Rob was on the phone asking for you. I was able to tell him that all went well. Maybe you can send him a wee text message once you wake up a bit.'

'Thanks, Glenda. I will.'

When the nurses have left and my breakfast tray is empty, I turn away from the window and curl up in a ball under my blanket. I'm tired and groggy and my head aches so badly it feels like it will explode.

The anaesthetic is still circulating. I fall asleep despite the pain.

I wake to a gentle voice calling me for lunch, and I stumble my way to the dining area.

Back in my room, my bed beckons to me. My head is still sore and I'm tired, but I really want to wash this egg out of my long hair. I take a towel from my cupboard.

The hot water refreshes me, but I still need to lie down again. I take my phone and send Rob a message: 'Thanks for phoning the ward, love. Head sore, but otherwise fine. Looking forward to seeing you later.'

He responds immediately: 'How are you feeling?'

He's so desperate for the ECT to have helped. I pause, trying to assess my mood. I haven't been crying today. I've eaten. Could I be a bit better? I write back: 'Maybe a little less depressed. I love you.'

The phone beeps again: 'I'm so glad to hear that. Love you too.'

What is electroconvulsive therapy (ECT)?

ECT involves sending a controlled electric current through the brain. This triggers a seizure which can relieve the symptoms of depression, mania or psychosis. It is carried out under general anaesthetic so that the patient has no awareness or memory of it, and muscle relaxants are used so that the body only twitches slightly rather than convulsing. A series of between six and twelve treatments is usually required.[1]

The Royal College of Psychiatrists runs an ECT Accreditation Service which carried out a study of ECT treatments in 2012–13. This showed that 1,712 in 1,789 people who had ECT improved 'minimally', 'much' or 'very much'.[2] It is also a safe treatment (the main risks are those associated with the general anaesthetic), though some memory loss is common.[3]

Four years. It has been four long years of looking to God and questioning what he is doing in our lives, and I feel as though I am beginning to draw some conclusions.

Three things now stand out for me in the middle of all my suffering and wrestling, towering above my doubts and fears:

- I am held.
- God is good.
- He gives me strength.

Simple truths, yet I have come to believe them and draw strength from them.

I am held

Psalm 139 keeps coming back to me. It reminds me that I am 'fearfully and wonderfully made' (verse 14) and teaches me to pray, asking God to 'search me . . . and know my heart' (verse 23).

But there are also the verses I had somehow completely missed:

Where can I go from your Spirit?
Where can I flee from your presence?
If I go up to the heavens, you are there.
If I make my bed in the depths, you are there.
If I rise on the wings of the dawn,

if I settle on the far side of the sea,
even there your hand will guide me,
your right hand will hold me fast.
(Psalm 139:7–10)

Even there. Even then. I had sometimes wondered how it was that I could come through so much and yet still feel God's presence. These verses remind me that God's right hand holds me fast – regardless of my circumstances.

When I ascend to the heights of mania and I can't express my faith in any constructive way, God is there.

When I fall into the pit of depression and my thoughts are disorganized and psychotic, God is there.

When I travelled across the ocean to have treatment at New Beginnings, God was there.

When I said that I hated him, and when I chose to attempt to end my life, even then God was there.

Not only is he here with me today, inspiring me as I write, but this psalm reminds me that he clasps me tightly in his right hand. And he has proven faithful through so much turmoil that I believe he will never let me go.

I am his. I am held. Even then. Even there.

God is good

The title of this book comes from the beginning of Psalm 13, which captures the angst of my struggle with mental illness:

How long, LORD? Will you forget me for ever?
How long will you hide your face from me?
How long must I wrestle with my thoughts
and day after day have sorrow in my heart?
How long will my enemy triumph over me?
(Psalm 13:1–2)

When David wrote this, he was clearly in psychological distress, defeated by his enemies and feeling as though God had forgotten him. He questioned God, but thoughtfully ... and his thoughts turned to the many times when God had proven faithful, rescuing and sustaining him. In time, his questioning was replaced by worship:

> But I trust in your unfailing love;
> my heart rejoices in your salvation.
> I will sing the Lord's praise,
> for he has been good to me.
> (Psalm 13:5–6)

Even in his wrestling, David could remember God's goodness.

My memory has been sharpened through the process of writing this book. I have suffered afresh the pain of the past as I have revisited times of despair, rejection, conflict, abandonment and fear – products of severe mental illness. Yet I have also reflected on the volume of evidence in my story that proves God's goodness to me.

But how can I say that God has been good to me? If I do a rewind, I can come up with twelve reasons:

- In my student days, he led me to a church where I was taught the Scriptures, a place where words of hope were instilled in me before my illness emerged, a place where I found love and fellowship, with friends (such as Lesley and Esther) remaining loyal to me as I transitioned painfully from doctor to patient.
- He put godly people around me, most notably my aunt, Olivia, who first recognized my depression in California and helped me to get the treatment I needed. She supported me through hospital admissions, made it possible for me to go to New Beginnings and – even still, at the time of writing – calls me every day from Los Angeles. Her presence in my life is a gift.
- He put me in an excellent medical school where I learned so much in my first four years that I was still able to pass my finals, despite missing so much teaching as a result of illness.

- God gave me psychiatrists in Belfast who recognized that I was critically unwell, admitted me to hospital, supported me through exams and worked to get me the best available treatment, even if going to London was ultimately unsuccessful.
- When I was floundering without support, he provided the opportunity for me to go to New Beginnings. There I was surrounded by loving Christians who gave me the help that I needed to overcome my eating disorder – including Rick, a therapist I could really trust.
- Back home, he gave me a GP, Dr Oates, who (along with her colleagues in the health centre) went above and beyond the call of duty, advocating for me until I got the psychiatric care that I needed. For six years, her calm, consistent presence in my life gave me untold reassurance. Without Dr Oates and Olivia, I truly believe I would not be here today.
- When I attempted suicide, he ensured that I was looked after by skilled physicians who addressed the medical issues but also cared enough to refer me directly to a psychiatrist, Dr Harris. She invested in me with twice-weekly therapy until I had the right diagnosis.
- During further admissions, he allowed hospital consultants to observe my symptoms over time until they were confident to make the diagnosis of schizoaffective disorder. This meant that my treatment could be optimized.
- God gave me back my stability, so that I could take on a job that I found fulfilling, and provided a supportive employer who did her best to understand my illness and needs.
- He blessed me with Rob, a chivalrous, witty, intelligent boyfriend who would become my steady, loving, patient husband. Many men would have walked away, but Rob endures many difficult days, inspired by the God he loves.
- In my new home at the coast, he has put me in a church where I hear his word taught, and where people care about me and want to learn about my illness. Here, I have met friends who make meals for Rob when I am in hospital; visit me; send care packages or flowers; take me out for coffee and chat; keep in touch with

me by phone and social media; and who, along with my Belfast friends, pray for me every day.

- In my new town, he has given me a Christian GP with an interest in mental illness, and perceptive psychiatrists and caring nurses – both in the community and in the inpatient unit where I have spent time. My drug regimen has been improved and the ECT I have undergone has also helped me.

Today, I walked my dogs along the beach against a backdrop of majestic mountains. I know that I have friends and family members to whom I can turn when I need a chat, and health professionals who are just a phone call away if I need more support than that. I am well enough to look after my home and to spend time writing in a café. I am having counselling I can manage my lingering depression.

I have hope. God is good.

He gives me strength

I recently heard a sermon on Psalm 46 about God, the Refuge of his people and Conqueror of the nations. The poetry of the psalm is strikingly beautiful, but I got stuck on the first verse, repeating it over and over again in my mind:

> God is our refuge and strength,
> an ever-present help in trouble.
> (Psalm 46:1)

It rings so true. My illness might weaken me, but the same God who holds me and is good to me gives me strength, and he has done so many, many times along this journey.

Strength:

- to admit that I was depressed and, with Olivia's support, to make that first GP appointment. To walk into the psychiatry outpatients department when all I wanted was to run away;

- to cope with the unfamiliar routine and unpredictable behaviour of other patients during my first inpatient admission in Belfast;
- to walk out of my ward and into the assessment centre, where I managed to pass my finals against all the odds;
- to survive two demoralizing hospital stays in London. To step into the unknown and begin treatment in the USA;
- to go back to church even though people were aware of my suicide attempt;
- to keep going through uncertain times until my doctors settled on a final diagnosis of schizoaffective disorder;
- to stick to my drug regimen even when I did start to feel better and became frustrated by sedation. To re-enter the workplace and carry out a responsible job;
- to start taking part in new social activities again – like the creative writing class where I met Rob;
- to try dating after so many years when I assumed that I would always be single;
- to commit to loving Rob for ever, to uproot from my home to live with him in Newcastle, County Down, and to stay there through days of loneliness when I would have moved back to Belfast in a heartbeat;
- to survive more hospital admissions to a different mental health unit, and to trust a new treatment team; to speak out when one psychologist was disrespectful about my faith;
- to try new medications, despite fears about their side effects, and to stick with them until they really began to help. To agree to ECT and to endure thirteen general anaesthetics in one year;
- to get up this morning, as I do every day, despite feeling that gnawing depression which never quite leaves me;
- to begin the daily routine and cope on my own while Rob is at work.

And, of course, strength to write my story. Strength to be open, honest, vulnerable. Strength to reach out and strengthen others who 'wrestle with thoughts', showing them that hope can be real.

Now that my story is written down, I can see ample evidence of my weakness, but that makes God's 'ever-present help in trouble' all the more obvious.

He is mighty. He gives me strength.

My journey through severe mental illness has been hard, and I know that I face a future that is likely to involve even more of the same struggles. If that was where the story ended, you would understand if I lived in a state of despair.

But I don't.

Instead, I rest in the knowledge that I will never fall from God's right hand. He has a proven record of goodness to me even in times of great pain, and he has upheld his promise to be my strength and my refuge.

* * *

The line is a little crackly. I move my phone over to my left ear.

'How are things today?'

Olivia's tone is bright. I can picture her driving between rows of Santa Monica palm trees on her way to the hospital.

'Mm, I'm okay. Still a bit low. Tired, you know?'

'I know. Hmmph! Uh, sorry – a cyclist just ignored a four-way stop. Hey!' I hear Olivia regulating her breathing.

'It was in the news today that they need to train a hundred more medical students every year in Northern Ireland to meet the demand for doctors.'

'Ha, and you thought you could fill a gap . . .'

'I can't help it. I wish there was a way for me to get back to medicine.'

Olivia sighs softly.

'Even now that you've uncovered your real passion?'

'My passion? You mean writing?'

'Of course.'

'Just because I've written my story doesn't mean I can write other things.'

'But, Sharon, you've always been a writer.'

'I know, but . . .'

I pause, look out of the window.

In the sense that I've always written things, she's right. I contributed to medical journals constantly when I was a student. Even at primary school, I used to tell people I was going to be an author.

'But I would have loved being a GP. And I think I could have been a good one.'

'You find it hard to let go, don't you?'

'It's one of the last things I am wrestling with – the idea that I will never be a doctor.'

'But you are a doctor. You write as a doctor.'

A doctor-writer. Maybe that's what God intends for me.

I am back at my baptism again.

Jesus, all for Jesus,
all I am and have and ever hope to be . . .
All of my ambitions, hopes and plans,
I surrender these into your hands . . .
For it's only in your will that I am free.
(Robin Mark)[4]

and we take captive every thought to make it obedient to Christ.
(2 Corinthians 10:5)

Epilogue

When I was in my late teens, I was a lieutenant in the Boys' Brigade. As the pianist who accompanied the boys' singing, I often played the official BB hymn, 'Will your anchor hold?' by Priscilla Owens. I had no idea how important its words would become:

Will your anchor hold in the storms of life,
when the clouds unfold their wings of strife?
When the strong tides lift, when the cables strain,
will your anchor drift, or firm remain?[1]

In the years since the Boys' Brigade, I have certainly known storms, cloudy days and strong tides. My 'boat' has been buffeted by waves of psychosis, the high winds of mania, and the relentless, lashing rain of depression.

But, despite my mental illness, as a follower of Jesus I can join in the refrain:

We have an anchor that keeps the soul
steadfast and sure while the billows roll;
fastened to the Rock which cannot move,
grounded firm and deep in the Saviour's love![2]

This chorus echoes the amazing words of reassurance in Hebrews 6:19: 'We have this hope as an anchor for the soul, firm and secure', and it sometimes plays in my head at times of deep struggle.

Yes, I am still riding the rough seas of schizoaffective disorder, and my life has become complicated by physical conditions which are exacerbated by some of the medication necessary to control my mood and my psychosis.

My mind is fractured; my body is weak. I am mentally and physically tired, and I often feel as if I could easily slide back into despair. And yet I have this assurance that – whatever the state of my mind and my body – my *soul* is secure, anchored to a 'Rock which cannot move'.

Because of this, I can answer the questions of the hymn's last stanza with a confident 'Yes!'

> Will your eyes behold through the morning light
> the city of gold and the harbour bright?
> Will you anchor safe by the heavenly shore,
> when life's storms are past for evermore?[3]

Schizoaffective disorder, like schizophrenia and bipolar disorder, is an enduring, lifelong condition. I have experienced a measure of healing – through the knowledge of God's right hand holding on to me, of his goodness and his strength, and through a medication regimen that has helped me function out of hospital – but I do not expect that I will be completely free from mental illness in my lifetime.

Yet I know that, at the end of my journey, I will anchor in the bright harbour of the heavenly city, and that's what really matters to me.

Then life's storms will be firmly in the past, and I will wrestle with my thoughts no more.

> God, who foresaw your tribulation, has specially armed you to go through it, not without pain, but without stain.
> (C. S. Lewis)[4]

> [God] will also keep you firm to the end, so that you will be blameless on the day of our Lord Jesus Christ.
> (1 Corinthians 1:8)

Appendix 1
Frequently asked questions

How do I get alongside someone at church who may have a severe mental illness?

People with mental illness are often on the fringes of church life. They may not be regular attenders at services or events. When you do see them, start by saying 'Hi' and introducing yourself. If you ask how they are, make it okay for them to be real. Something along the lines of 'I'm glad to get this coffee – it's been a difficult week. How are you?' can help. Choose a low-key church event and ask them if they'd like to go with you, or suggest meeting up for a chat at a local café. Win their trust by sticking around; introduce them to some others, and you may find that they are drawn in from the margins.

How can I support someone who uses psychiatric services?

First of all, normalize their experience. If you talk about their visit to a mental health service provider, approach the conversation just as you would if they were seeing someone about their physical health. Affirm the role of psychiatrists and mental health professionals in the lives of Christians – they are doctors who treat illness of the brain, and their commonly used therapies are consistent with Scripture (remember CBT and 'take captive every thought' in 2 Corinthians 10:5?). Find out if you can support them practically – offer transport to appointments, or offer to attend with them if they are nervous or find it difficult to remember things. And, of course, pray for them.

What can I do to help if someone is admitted to hospital with mental health problems?

People are often nervous about visiting a mental health unit for the first time, but there really is no need to be. It is a bit different from visiting a general ward – you meet the patient in a communal area rather than at the bedside, and nurses will check anything you bring for the patient in case it could pose a risk (such as a plastic bag or a glass vase). It is a very important ministry, for days spent in a mental health unit can be long, and patients will appreciate time spent with someone they already know – a friend or a pastor. You might share a couple of Bible verses that have been meaningful to you at hard times, or simply sit in silent solidarity. Let carers/family know that you are visiting. It may give them a night off to recharge their batteries.

If you can't visit, think about sending a cheery card or a bunch of flowers, for example; keep in touch with the patient using messaging apps; see if you can make a meal for a carer; and, of course, pray!

How can my church help to dispel the stigma around mental health issues?

Start by making mental health and well-being as much a part of conversations as physical health. If a minister is preaching on a passage where a biblical character is struggling, he or she can bring out the importance of looking after mental health and how God cares for the 'poor in spirit' (Matthew 5:3). Pray publicly for those who are depressed, anxious or living with bipolar disorder or schizophrenia (without mentioning names unless agreed in advance), and for mental health professionals. You might have a special service for World Mental Health Day, inviting a Christian psychiatrist or counsellor to speak. If you have a book review slot, feature a book about mental illness (see Appendix 2 for some ideas), and encourage youth and family workers to attend training on mental health issues. Be open about your own struggles – breaking stigma is contagious!

How can my church reach out to individuals with severe mental illness in the community?

Learn to locate people with bipolar or psychotic illness. There may be a 'supported living' housing complex in your area, or a charity may host a local day centre for people with mental health problems. Find out if volunteers are needed – church members may be able to share their crocheting or woodwork skills with a group of service users, or simply be around to have a chat over a cup of tea. If a local counselling or crisis centre is having a fundraiser, take part in the sponsored walk/cycle/abseil, or bake something for the cake sale, and use the opportunity to fight stigma at the same time. Consider opening a church drop-in once a week for those who struggle with mental health problems, or simply offer your facilities for a support group to use without cost. Such faith-in-action gestures will help people to feel comfortable with the church, and in time some may even try going to a service.

Does a believer with severe mental illness need a Christian psychiatrist/nurse/ professional?

As we have seen, psychiatrists are skilled doctors who use medication and other therapies to treat illnesses of the brain. In that sense, it is no more important to a Christian that the professional is a believer than if he or she was a rheumatologist or a gastric surgeon. I have never been cared for by a Christian psychiatrist in this country, yet I have benefited from the expertise of all those who have been involved in my care. Mental health professionals are trained to respect patients' faith, and 'spirituality' is increasingly considered when assessing someone's well-being. Having said that, I once had to stop working with a psychologist whose views on Christianity were so opposed to mine that we reached an impasse, so it is worth being aware that this can happen. We should pray for our mental health teams, regardless of whether they share our beliefs or not.

Aside from this, I do think it is helpful to have someone who is a Christian involved in one's mental health care, and I have found Christian counselling invaluable in this regard. Qualified and accredited Christian counsellors can be found through the Association of Christian Counsellors (<www.acc-uk.org/>).

Should a Christian take 'mind-altering' drugs?

Psychiatric drugs have a clear evidence base for the treatment of severe depression, psychosis, bipolar disorder, schizophrenia and other mental illnesses.[1] In other words, like insulin for diabetes or amoxicillin for a chest infection, they work. In mental illness, neurotransmitter systems in the brain are over- or under-active, and drugs can help to restore the balance. If we treat other brain and central nervous system disorders – such as Parkinson's disease and multiple sclerosis – with medication, it makes sense to use medication to treat mental illnesses too. Indeed, the line dividing neurology and psychiatry is blurring. I can say from personal experience that 'mind-altering' drugs have improved my ability to connect with God, freeing me from symptoms that consumed me, and allowing me to gain the stability I need to practise my faith.

How do I know the difference between psychotic illness and demon possession?

This is a big question, requiring more space and nuance than a book of this nature can fully address, but one that does come up, so I have compiled a few thoughts.

The Bible leaves us in no doubt that demon possession exists, and Jesus made it part of his disciples' mission both to 'drive out all demons and to cure diseases' (Luke 9:1), but the Bible also speaks often of mental illness. For example, fearing for his life, David 'feigned insanity . . . he acted like a madman . . . letting saliva run down his beard' (1 Samuel 21:13–14).

One key difference between the 'madmen' of the Bible and those who had demons is that the resident demons always recognized Jesus for who he was: 'Moreover, demons came out of many people, shouting, "You are the Son of God!"' (Luke 4:41). I have met many people with severe psychotic illness, and they have never seen Christ in me. I have written of my own experience of tormentors and evil presences, but these have never called out when I have entered a church, and they disappear when I take antipsychotic medication. I have psychosis – I am 'mad', not demon-possessed – and prayers for 'deliverance' have actually damaged me.

We must pray for discernment and seek advice from an expert (such as a Christian psychiatrist) before 'diagnosing' someone with demon possession. It is important not to add to the stigma and exclusion experienced by someone who is mentally ill. In the end, all illness – physical and mental – is the result of the Fall in Genesis, when humankind sinned, and, in that sense, is a consequence of evil.

We are thankful, then, for Jesus, our great Redeemer, who will one day usher in a new order where there is '"no more death" or mourning or crying or pain' (Revelation 21:4). A world without mental illness will be heaven indeed.

Appendix 2
Useful contacts and resources

Web resources with downloadable leaflets and information on a range of mental illnesses, including schizophrenia, bipolar disorder and schizoaffective disorder:

Mind
'The mental health charity'
<www.mind.org.uk>

Rethink Mental Illness
'A better life for everyone affected by mental illness.'
<www.rethink.org>

The Royal College of Psychiatrists (UK)
Advice from a medical perspective.
<www.rcpsych.ac.uk/mental-health>

Online advice from a Christian viewpoint

Biblical Counselling UK

Mind and Soul Foundation
'To equip, educate and encourage.'

Think Twice

'To increase awareness and decrease stigma so that people are as able to be open about their mental health condition as they are about having the flu.'
<www.thinktwiceinfo.org>

Helpful books

Elyn R. Saks, *The Centre Cannot Hold: My Journey through Madness* (New York: Hachette Books, 2007). A professor of law at the University of Southern California writes of her schizophrenia, and how it has changed her life and work. Hope for anyone who has endured psychotic illness.

Kay Redfield Jamison, *An Unquiet Mind: A Memoir of Moods and Madness* (London: Picador, 1995). Kay Redfield Jamison is a professor of psychiatry at the Johns Hopkins University School of Medicine. She also suffers from bipolar disorder. She writes of her 'war with lithium' and her ultimate acceptance of an illness that makes her 'feel more things, more deeply'.

Kathryn Greene-McCreight, *Darkness Is My Only Companion: A Christian Response to Mental Illness* (Grand Rapids: Brazos Press, 2015). A renowned theologian, Greene-McCreight writes, 'This project examines the distress caused and the Christian theological questions raised by a clinical mental illness, namely, mine.' Her struggle with bipolar disorder informs her academic reflections. Brutally honest, immediate and true.

Mark Meynell, *When Darkness Seems My Closest Friend: Reflections on Life and Ministry with Depression* (London: IVP, 2018). A Christian minister, speaker and writer seeks to find words for those whose depressive illness has left them speechless. Not only a highly personal account of a journey through illness, but also a compendium of resources for 'fellow cave-dwellers'.

Alan Thomas, *Tackling Mental Illness Together: A Biblical and Practical Approach* (London: IVP, 2017). A professor of psychiatry offers wise advice to Christians who are not mental health professionals but want to make a difference for those who have mental illness. Accessible and empowering.

Emma Scrivener, *A New Name: Grace and Healing for Anorexia* (London: IVP, 2012); *A New Day: Moving on from Hunger, Anxiety, Control, Shame, Anger and Despair* (London: IVP, 2017). Beautifully written accounts of finding Jesus amid an agonizing personal struggle with mental illness, combined with practical tools for readers for whom Emma's story is all too familiar.

In an emergency

If you or someone else is at serious risk, call 999 or attend your nearest Accident and Emergency Department.

If the situation is less urgent, see your GP or contact your local out-of-hours service. In England and Wales, phone 111.

For immediate emotional support

Premier Lifeline: this National Christian Helpline provides confidential emotional and spiritual support from a Christian per-spective. Call 0300 111 0101 between 9 am and midnight.

The Samaritans provide twenty-four-hour telephone (116 123) and email (jo@samaritans.org) helplines.

Notes

Epigraph

1 C. S. Lewis, *The Problem of Pain* (Glasgow: Collins, Fount Paperbacks, 1940, reprinted 1983), p. 144.

Introduction: Deep joy

1 Robin Mark, 'All for Jesus'. All lyrics from the song quoted in this introduction are used by kind permission.

1 Too numb to pray: Wrestling with thoughts of darkness

1 'Depression', Royal College of Psychiatrists, June 2015, available at <www.rcpsych.ac.uk/mental-health/problems-disorders/depression>.
2 'Depression', Royal College of Psychiatrists, June 2015.
3 'Depression', Royal College of Psychiatrists, June 2015.
4 'Depression', Royal College of Psychiatrists, June 2015.

2 The symphonies have lost their colour: Wrestling with low mood

1 'Other Specified Feeding or Eating Disorder (OFSED)', Beat Eating Disorders, available at <www.beateatingdisorders.org.uk/types/osfed>.
2 'Other Specified Feeding or Eating Disorder (OFSED)', Beat Eating Disorders.

3 'I want to go home': Wrestling with my loss of freedom

1 'The Mental Health Act 1983', Rethink Mental Illness, available at <www.rethink.org/living-with-mental-illness/mental-health-laws/mental-health-act-1983>.

'Guidelines on the use of the Mental Health (Northern Ireland) Order 1986', Guidelines and Audit Implementation Network, available at <https://bit.ly/2RSsRWf>.

4 Throwing the bouquet in the bin: Wrestling with my identity

1 'Cognitive Behavioural Therapy (CBT)' (online factsheet), Royal College of Psychiatrists, available at <www.rcpsych.ac.uk/mental-health/treatments-and-wellbeing/cognitive-behavioural-therapy-(cbt)>.

2 A. Szentagotai and D. David, 'The efficacy of cognitive-behavioural therapy in bipolar disorder: a quantitative meta-analysis', *Journal of Clinical Psychiatry*, 2010; 71(1): 66–72, DOI: 10.4088/JCP.08r04559yel.
Emmanuelle Peters et al., 'The long-term effectiveness of cognitive behaviour therapy for psychosis within a routine psychological therapies service', *Frontiers in Psychology*, 2015; 6: 1658, DOI: 10.3389/fpsyg.2015.01658.

7 Sighing out my bitterness: Wrestling with despair

1 John 10:27–28.

8 Too alive: Wrestling with suicidal thoughts

1 K. M. Holma et al., 'Incidence and predictors of suicide attempts in DSM-IV major depressive disorder: a five-year prospective study', *American Journal of Psychiatry*, 2010; 167(7): 801–8.

2 C. Crump, K. Sundquist and M. A. Winkleby, 'Bipolar disorder: a Swedish national cohort study', *JAMA* 2013; 70(9): 931–9.

3 S. G. Siris, 'Suicide and schizophrenia', *Journal of Psychopharmacology*, 2001; 15(2): 127–35.

9 Aftercare. At last: Wrestling with my body

1 'What is psychoanalytic psychotherapy?', British Psychoanalytic Council, available at <www.bpc.org.uk/about-psychotherapy/what-psychotherapy>.

2 Bent Rosenbaum et al., 'Supportive psychodynamic psychotherapy versus treatment as usual for first-episode psychosis: two-year outcome', *Psychiatry*, 2012; 75 (4).

10 More than well: Wrestling with mania

1 'Good King Wenceslas', John Mason Neale, 1853.

2 'Bipolar disorder: overview', National Institute of Mental Health, April 2016, available at <www.nimh.nih.gov/health/topics/bipolar-disorder/index.shtml>.

3 P. K. Chaudhury, K. Deka and D. Chetia, 'Disability associated with mental disorders', *Indian Journal of Psychiatry*, 2006; 48(2): 95–101.

4 C. Crump, K. Sundquist and M. A. Winkleby, 'Bipolar disorder: a Swedish national cohort study', *JAMA*, 2013; 70(9): 931–9.

5 Crump, Sundquist and Winkleby, 'Bipolar disorder: a Swedish national cohort study'.

6 'Hypomania and mania', Mind, August 2016, available at <www.mind.org.uk/information-support/types-of-mental-health-problems/hypomania-and-mania/#.Wl4a-Khl82w>.

7 'Hypomania and mania', Mind, August 2016.

8 'What is bipolar disorder?' Mind, May 2018, available at <www.mind.org.uk/information-support/types-of-mental-health-problems/bipolar-disorder/#.XYxymShKiUl>.

9 'What is bipolar disorder?' Mind.

10 'What is bipolar disorder?' Mind.

12 The network in the fourth dimension: Wrestling with psychosis

1 'Early psychosis and psychosis', National Alliance on Mental Illness, US, available at <www.nami.org/Learn-More/Mental-Health-Conditions/Related-Conditions/Psychosis>.

2 'Schizophrenia', Royal College of Psychiatrists, available at <www.rcpsych.ac.uk/mental-health/problems-disorders/schizophrenia>.

3 'Schizophrenia', World Health Organization, available at <www.who.int/topics/schizophrenia/en/>.

4 'Schizophrenia', Royal College of Psychiatrists.

5 'Schizoaffective disorder', National Alliance on Mental Illness, available at <www.nami.org/learn-more/mental-health-conditions/schizoaffective-disorder>.

6 J. Perala et al., 'Lifetime prevalence of psychotic and bipolar I disorders in a general population', archives of *JAMA Psychiatry*, 2007; 64(1): 19–28.

7 Chin-Kuo Chang et al., 'Life expectancy at birth for people with serious mental illness and other major disorders from a secondary mental health care case register in London', *PLoS One*, 18 May 2011, available at <doi.org/10.1371/journal.pone.0019590>.

8 W. Carpenter and H. Wehring, 'Violence and schizophrenia', *Schizophrenia Bulletin*, September 2011.

14 This doesn't feel like 'friends': Wrestling with risk

1 Ruth Trimble, 'Let you go', used by kind permission.

16 Even there your hand will guide: Wrestling, with acceptance

1 'Electroconvulsive Therapy (ECT)', Mind, available at <www.mind.org.uk/information-support/drugs-and-treatments/electroconvulsive-therapy-ect/#.XFA5VVz7Q2w>.

2 'Electroconvulsive Therapy (ECT)', Mind.

3 'Efficacy and safety of electroconvulsive therapy in depressive disorders: a systematic review and meta-analysis', UK ECT Review Group, *Lancet*, 2003; 361(9360): 799–808

4 Robin Mark, 'All for Jesus', used by kind permission.

Epilogue

1 Priscilla Owens (1829–1907), 'Will your anchor hold in the storms of life?' (public domain).

2 Owens, 'Will your anchor hold in the storms of life?'

3 Owens, 'Will your anchor hold in the storms of life?'

4 C. S. Lewis, 'Letter to Mrs Lockley' in Walter Hooper (ed.), *The Collected Letters of C. S. Lewis* Volume II (San Francisco: HarperSanFrancisco, 2004), p. 975.

Appendix 1: Frequently asked questions

1 S. Leucht, S. Hierl, W. Kissling et al., 'Putting the efficacy of psychiatric and general medicine medication into perspective: review of meta-analyses', *British Journal of Psychiatry*, 2012; 200: 97–106.

Appendix 1: Frequently asked questions

At the age of six, Sharon Hastings self-published her first book: *The Long Train Went under the Bridge*, held together with staples. Writing has always been a big part of her life. She told her teachers that she wanted to be an author when she grew up, and that dream never really left her, even when her love of people and her desire to help them drew her towards a career in medicine.

As a medical student, Sharon wrote for magazines and websites, and notably saw her 'History of Gastric Surgery in Belfast' (a collaborative effort with her uncle, a surgeon) published in the *Ulster Medical Journal*. And when poor health got in the way of practising as a doctor, Sharon attended creative writing classes, which was where she met her husband, Robert, a video producer and budding sci-fi author who has become her primary carer and greatest cheerleader.

Despite her struggle with severe mental illness, Sharon graduated with a degree in Medicine and a Certificate in Counselling from Queen's University, Belfast, in 2007. She went on to achieve a Postgraduate Certificate in Clinical Education and taught anatomy briefly at the university before moving into Constituency Casework roles in the offices of three successive elected representatives.

The schizoaffective disorder that first emerged when she was at medical school affects every aspect of Sharon's life, but her faith remains central to her journey. Pastoral support is as important to her as the vital ongoing input from mental health professionals, and in *Wrestling with My Thoughts* she writes about encountering God in the midst of depression, mania and psychosis.

When she is well, Sharon enjoys life in Newcastle, County Down, with Rob, their two golden retrievers and a loyal one-eyed cat. Her interests include live music, Bible study and walking by the sea. At the time of writing, she is working part-time, but considers her ministry through the written word of paramount importance, just as she did when first stapling her 'books' together in 1988.